THE HISTORY OF HIP HOP

COLLECTION

ERIC REESE

Copyright © 2017-2020 by Eric Reese

All rights reserved.

No part of this book may be reproduced in any form or by any electronic or mechanical means, including information storage and retrieval systems, without written permission from the author, except for the use of brief quotations in a book review.

ISBN: 9781925988574

For all the real fans of Hip-Hop worldwide!

CONTENTS

VOLUME ONE

Introduction	3
1980's	7
80's Style	9
90's Purpose	11
90's Interpretation of Music	13
The Plight of Hip Hop	15
Social Connection	17
Politics	19
Hip-Hop is Art	21
Motive	23
Texture	25
Worldwide	27
Urban Fashion	29
Innovation and Revitalization	31
Rise of Hip-Hop in the 2000's	33
What Purpose does Hip-Hop serve?	35
History: 1925 - 2000	37
Moments in Pop Culture History	55
Terminology	65
The Term: Hip-Hop	67
Seventies' Roots of Hip-Hop	69
Influence of Disco	73
Transition to Recording	75
Nationalization & Internationalization	79
Early New School	81
The Golden Age	83
Gangsta Rap & West Coast	85

World Hip Hop	87
Glimpses of West Coast Hip Hop	91
Glimpses of East Coast Hip Hop	93
Diversification of Styles	97
Across the World	101
Glitch Hop and Wonky Music	105
Crunk and Snap Music	107

VOLUME TWO

Introduction	111
1. Elements of Hip-Hop	115
2. Hip-Hop through the years	119
3. Definition of Rapping	125
4. Hip Hop's Trendsetting Groups	131
5. 80's Hip Hop Artists	143
6. Top Hip-Hop Songs of the 1980s	149
7. Top Hip-Hop Albums of the 1980s	167
1980	197
1981	205
1982	211
1983	217
1984	229
1985	247
1986	259
1987	277
1988	287
1989	297

VOLUME THREE

Introduction	309
1. Hip Hop At A Glance	311
2. Review of the Elements of Hip Hop	313

3. Elements of B-boying   321
4. Elements of Graffiti Culture   325
5. 1990s   331
6. Hip Hop History (1990-1999)   341
7. What is Hip Hop? (Revisited)   353
8. Hip Hop and the Youth   359
9. Culture of Hip Hop and Social Consciousness   365
10. Hip Hop Impacting All   375

   Afterword   383

VOLUME ONE

INTRODUCTION

What is Hip Hop? The word can mean many things to different people. To some, it is a lifestyle. To others, it is simply a genre of music - revered by some, and dismissed by others. One thing is for sure: Hip Hop has a lengthy history, which audibly and visibly tells the story of thousands of inner-city lives. So, where exactly did it come from?

Hip Hop established its roots in the 1970's in New York City, specifically, largely African-American parts of the Bronx and Brooklyn. DJs were using turntables to create music that was fused from separate records. They would create a rhythm using these "beats" and create lyrical poetry over the spliced sounds to make what is the essential foundation of all hip hop and rap music today.

Since these early days, Hip Hop has expanded quite a

INTRODUCTION

bit. While it was originally a form of musical poetry (so to speak), it has developed several subgenres such as "crunk", "gangsta rap", and more. Crunk music, or crunk rap, is a style of Hip-Hop that developed in the southern United States. Its loud anthems and crowd-oriented singalongs are developed specifically to get the dancefloor moving. Gangsta Rap developed in the late eighties in Los Angeles and New York City and was centralized on hard beats which narrated life in the ghetto.

Between the mid-1980s and the early 1990s, hip-hop began to go through a metamorphosis. The art of MCing began to grow as artists started paying more attention to song structure with 4-bar choruses and 16-bar verses, and descriptive narrations in raps.

Early rap pacesetters used wordplay. MCs branched away from end-rhymes rhyming couplets and began different literary approaches such as internal rhyme and chain rhyme. Hip-Hop transitioned from the break beat to characteristics of soul, funk, and jazz.

When major labels began to seek out artists, Hip-Hop drastically grew and entered television media on programs such as MTV and BET. Run from the hip-hop legends known as Run-DMC was once quoted saying, "At a time when hip-hop was becoming really popular in all five boroughs in New York, Bambaataa, Grandmaster Flash, everybody started dressin' up 'cause they had a little bit of money. The Cold Crush Brothers would just come to the parties as is and do their performance."

Since its inception in the seventies, Hip Hop has seen considerable change and evolution. While it comes in many forms, hip hop will always serve as a looking glass to the outside world into African-American culture - for better or for worse. As it continues to change through the 2000's, hip hop will forever stand as both a lifestyle and a style of music which pays homage to its culture throughout over thirty years of history.

1980'S

Rap did not really come in to play until the 1980's because of the dominance of disco. Because of hardships and inequality, young men who had more talent than money put bits and pieces of everybody tracks while putting their poetry on top of their agendas. The B-Boys were from the ghetto, while disco was for the middle class and the rich. But there was hip-hop in both worlds. It was the Hip-Hop tug-o'-war -- disco rappers versus the B-Boys. The '80s marked a new reality: East meets west, with the new, California-based breed seemingly taking their counterparts to the cleaners, businesswise and sales wise. The 80's brought a new innovative sound and cultural influence to Hip-Hop community and was known as the "Golden Age" era of Hip Hop. Famous artists from this era include Run D-M-C, Public Enemy, Slick Rick, Salt-N-Peppa, and Big Daddy Kane.

In 1981, Africka Bambaataa revolutionized the sound of Hip-Hop by making an Electro-funk beat to the song "Planet Rock". This fostered similar creativity throughout the Hip Hop world as other artists created their own style of music such as rap group Run DMC, who created "Rap Rock" (A fuse of vocal and instrumental Hip Hop elements combined with forms of Rock-N-Roll). This creative innovation during the 80's is how the name "Golden Age" came about.

In the 1980s, Hip-Hop focused less on the political and marketing aspect on the music industry and more on the lyrical content and overall quality of music. For example, prior to the institution of royalty fees for using snippets of pre-recorded music, rappers were given way more creative freedom because they were able to sample. *"Corporate greed killed the creative music spirit in Hip Hop."*

80'S STYLE

Early female hip-hop artists such as Roxanne Shante, MC Late and Queen Latifah influenced fashion trends for women. Also, the film "Breakin' and Breakin' 2: Electric Boogaloo" showed people what to wear and what slang to say in order to be "hip." Rappers in general during that time wore leather, buttons, bracelets, and chains. Hip Hop artists tended to wear excessive large gold jewelry in the 80's, along with the large outbreak of people wearing basketball sneakers (such as Air Jordans and Adidas shelltops) for recreational and fashionable purposes.

Afro-centrism and the Nation of Islam expanded tremendously in the 1980s, so an increasing amount of African-American males wore Kente cloth. Females in the Hip Hop community wore enormous gold earrings to represent prestige and wealth along with bright neon-colored clothing. Color blocking (design scheme of combining different colors and materials into a single garment) was introduced into the Hip-Hop community in the 80's.

The "Hi-Top" Fade was a very popular haircut in the 80's that was introduced into the urban community.

90'S PURPOSE

"Thematically, hip-hop began pushing beyond the partly rhymes and battle raps that had dominated its early life to include everything from Black Nationalist politics to Five-Percenter ideology to streetwise chronicles of the the criminal underground."

YALE (THE ANTHOLOGY OF RAP)

Hip-Hop in the 1990s served as a platform to tell a political and social story or to prove yourself as being an African-American.

90'S INTERPRETATION OF MUSIC

Rakim brought the deeper meanings of rap. The rhythms of Jazz were making their way into music. They used a lot of metaphors. For example, instead of using an deserted image of a drug, Rakim in "Microphone Fiend" creates a song around a metaphor: *"I was a fiend before I became teen, I melted microphones instead instead of cones of ice cream"*. It was one of the best rap songs ever.

THE PLIGHT OF HIP HOP

Hip-hop emerged out of a culture that had an atmosphere of disappointment. After WWII, there were many black refugees that settled in urban centers across America. An urban center in the city of the Bronx, NYC started Hip-hop. Young people also gathered together in parks to rap over sounds and other melodies. Rapping was at the center of this culture, but Hip-Hop was more than just the music.

SOCIAL CONNECTION

Hip-Hop was seen as an outlet for people of color's anger. They were angry because they were poor, black, disenfranchised, abused, ignored, etc. At this point in time, racial tensions were still on the rise. People of color were angry at mainly the middle and upper-class whites because they were mainly denied inclusion in the modern-day's society resulting in unfair wages and good-paying jobs.

POLITICS

Majority of politicians were rich, white males. Issues of segregation were still apparent, though the Civil Rights Era was basically over. Good economic opportunities were very hard to come by in the inner- cities, because all the whites moved out to the suburbs with their big businesses. This caused major issues for the poor who either had to travel long distances to find a good-paying job or resort to working for less wages.

HIP-HOP IS ART

Urban or street art that revolved around Hip-Hop during the 1980s was generally not accepted by the majority. Graffiti is Hip-Hop and police and many community residents saw it as vandalism. What they didn't realize that a new generation of urban folk saw it as art.

MOTIVE

The primary motive behind hip-hop was to express the anger of the people of color with the system and the "man." Artist used their music to draw attention to the plights of social justice and issues that needed to be fixed.

TEXTURE

In the beginning, rap artists generally rapped to artificial beats (beatboxing) and borrowed melodies. It revolved around the production of sounds, not the arrangement of instruments until the late 1970s.

WORLDWIDE

- One of the countries outside the US where hip-hop is most popular is the United Kingdom.

- Hip Hop has globalized into many cultures worldwide, as evident through the emergence of numerous regional graffiti art scenes.

- Hip Hop has emerged globally as a cultural movement based upon the roots of Hip Hop culture; strife and struggle.

- Hip-hop's inspiration differs depending on culture and location.

- All rap artists worldwide have in common is that they acknowledge African Americans in New York as being the inventors of its art.

- Hip-Hop is sometimes taken for granted by Americans, it is not so elsewhere, especially in the developing world, where it has come to represent the empowerment of the disenfranchised and a slice of getting to the American Dream.

URBAN FASHION

Extra baggy clothes, jerseys, shiny gold jewelry, grills, tank tops, do-rags, tracksuits, bucket hats, basketball caps were the trends in the early days. Nowadays, artists have tattoos, fitted pants, half-shaven heads, track jackets, shirts with sleeves and printed tees, snapbacks, baseball jackets, Jordans, Vans, Nike SB, and hoodies. Artists also have made brands like Gucci, Michael Kors, Fendi, and Louis Vuitton popular amongst the hip hop community.

INNOVATION AND REVITALIZATION

With the use of music distribution through the internet, many alternative rap artists find fans by far-reaching audiences on Soundcloud, Spotify, Amazon and other music distribution channels. Hip Hop artists such as Kid Cudi and Drake have managed to attain chart-topping hit songs, "Day 'n' Night" and "Best I Ever Had" respectively, by releasing their music on free online mixtapes without the help of a major record label.

Wale, J. Cole, Lupe Fiasco, The Cool Kids, Jay Electronica, and B.o.B have been noted by critics as expressing eclectic sounds, life experiences, and emotions rarely seen in mainstream hip hop.

Hip-hop is also used in modern-day rock songs as well.

Kanye West, Jay-Z, OutKast, Tupac, and Eminem are

some of the best-selling artists ever. Many of their collaborations involve a combination of hip-hop, pop, soul and R & B artists which has grossed millions.

RISE OF HIP-HOP IN THE 2000'S

- The popularity of hip hop music continues through the 2000s.

- Dr. Dre remained one of the most prominent hip hop figures in producing and beat-making in the beginning of the millennium.

- Dre is the one responsible for the fame of Marshall Mather's (Eminem).

- Hip Hop influences also found their way increasingly into mainstream pop during this period

- Crunk music gained considerable popularity via the likes of Lil Jon and the Ying Yang Twins.

- Jay-Z represented the cultural triumph of hip hop of the 2000s.

- Success of alternative Hip-Hop from groups like the Roots, Dilated Peoples, Gnarls Barkley and Mos Def gained notoriety.

WHAT PURPOSE DOES HIP-HOP SERVE?

Hip Hop gave young black men a voice to be heard especially when media technology started to become more feasible. Rapping also gave some the opportunity to do more than just commit crimes to survive.

Along with focusing on Black Nationalism, hip hop artists often talked about inner-city poverty. This brought a great deal of listeners to the genre who were struggling and coping with the scourge of alcohol, drugs, and gangs in their communities.

Public Enemy's most influential song came out at the time of one of the most plighted times in America called "Fight the Power." The song speaks up to the US government proclaiming that people in the ghetto have the freedom of speech and rights like any other American. One line in the song by Public Enemy, *"We got to pump the stuff to make us tough from the heart,"* grasped the listeners attention and gave them motivation to speak out.

HISTORY: 1925 - 2000

If you start in the past and work all the way to the present, the history of Hip-Hop spreads out in every direction. It dates back to the 1920s when the earliest hip hop dance movements were introduced in the nightclubs and on TV shows. Then it hit the Jamaican dancehall toasting era of the 1950s and 60s. Thus, spreading to the era of the Last Poets and Muhammad Ali and Gil Scott-Heron, who recited poems over beats. Then you had the golden ages of Rakim, Kool G Rap, LL Cool J of the 80s until Nas, Prodigy from Mob-Deep, Jay-Z of the 1990s and currently Jadakiss and Dave East.

1925:
Earl Tucker (aka Snake Hips), a performer at the Cotton Club, invents a dance style similar to today's hip-hop moves. He incorporates floats and slides into

his dance. Similar moves would later inspire an element of hip-hop culture known as breakdancing.

1940:
Tom the Great (a.k.a. Thomas Wong) uses a booming sound system to delight his audience. Wong also utilizes hip American records to steal music-lovers from competitors and local bands.

1950:
The Soundclash contest between Coxsone Dodd's "Downbeat" and Duke Reid's "Trojan" gives birth to the concept of DJ battling.

1956:
Clive Campbell is born in Kingston, Jamaica. (Campbell would later become the father of what we now know as hip-hop.)

1959:
Parks Commissioner Robert Moses starts building an expressway in the Bronx. Consequently, middle-class Germans, Irish, Italians, and Jewish, neighborhoods gradually disappear. Businesses relocate away from the borough only to be replaced by impoverished African-American and Hispanic families. Along with the poor came addiction, crime, and unemployment.

1962:

James Brown records Live At The Apollo. Brown's drummer Clayton Fillyau introduces a sound that is now known as the break beat. The break beat would later inspire the b-boy movement, as breakers danced to these beats at block parties.

1967:
Clive Campbell migrates to the United States at the age of 11. Because of his imposing size, kids at Alfred E. Smith High School nickname him Hercules. He would later become a graf writer and change his name to Kool Herc.

1968:
A gang named Savage Seven would hit the streets of the East Bronx. Savage Seven later changes its name to Black Spades, before eventually becoming an organization known as the Zulu Nation.

1969:
James Brown records two songs that would further influence the drum programming in today's rap music – "Sex Machines" with John Starks playing drums and "Funky Drummer" with Clyde Stubblefield on the drums.

1970:
DJ U-Roy invades Jamaican pop charts with three top ten songs using a style known as toasting. The Last Poets release their self-titled debut album on Douglas Records

combining jazz instrumentations with heartfelt spoken word. (The Last Poets would later appear on Common's 2005 rap anthem, "The Corner.")

1971:
Aretha Franklin records a well-known b-boy song "Rock Steady." The Rock Steady crew would go on to rule in the world of break-dancing, with members all across the globe.

1972:
The Black Messengers (a group that staged performances for The Black Panthers and rallies relating to black power movement) feature on The Gong Show.
However, they are only allowed to perform under the alias "Mechanical Devices," because of their controversial name.

1973:
DJ Kool Herc deejays his first block party (his sister's birthday) at 1520 Sedgwick Avenue, Bronx, NY. Herc would often buy two copies of a record and stretch the break parts by using two turntables and mixing in both records before the break ends. The Zulu Nation is officially formed by a student of Stevenson High school named Kevin Donovan. Donovan later changed his name to Afrika Bambaataa Aasim in honor of an ancient Zulu chief.

1974:
After seeing DJ Kool Herc perform at block parties, Grandmaster Caz, Grandmaster Flash, and Afrika Bambaataa start playing at parties all over the Bronx neighborhoods. Around this time, DJ/MC/Crowd Pleaser Lovebug Starski starts referring to this culture as "Hip-Hop."

1975:
Herc is hired as a DJ at the Hevalo Club.
He later gets Coke La Rock to utter crowd-pleasing rhymes at parties (e.g. "DJ Riz is in the house and he'll turn it out without a doubt"). Coke La Rock and Clark Kent form the first emcee team known as Kool Herc & The Herculoids. DJ Grand Wizard Theodore accidentally invents 'the scratch.' While trying to hold a spinning record in place in order to listen to his mom, who was yelling at him, Grand Wizard accidentally caused the record to produce the "shigi-shigi" sound that is now known as the scratch. Scratch is the crux of modern deejaying.

1976:
DJ Afrika Bambaataa performs at the Bronx River Center. Bambaataa's first battle against Disco King Mario sparks off the DJ battling that is now embedded in the culture.

1977:

The Rock Steady Crew (the most respected b-boy crew in history) is formed by the original four members: JoJo, Jimmy Dee, Easy Mike, and P-Body. DJ Kool Herc is nearly stabbed to death at one of his parties. Although the assault placed a permanent dent on Herc's career, Grandmaster Flash, Afrika Bambaataa, Disco Wiz (the first Latino DJ), and Disco King Mario kept performing around town.

1978:
Kurtis Blow, who was being managed by Russell Simmons, decides to hire Simmons' brother Run, as his DJ. Run was so-called because he could cut so fast between two turntables.
Kurtis would later become the first rapper to be signed to a major record deal.
Music industry coins the term "rap music" and shifts its focus toward emcees. Grandmaster Caz (aka Cassanova Fly) and Bambaataa engage in a battle at the Police Athletic League.

1979:
Grandmaster Flash forms one of the most influential rap groups ever, The Furious 5: Grandmaster Flash (Joseph Saddler), Melle Mel (Melvin Glover), Kidd Creole (Nathaniel Glover), Cowboy (Keith Wiggins), Raheim (Guy Williams), and Mr. Ness (Eddie Morris). Around the same time, another great rap crew – The Cold Crush Four – was formed, comprising of Charlie Chase, Tony

Tone, Grand Master Caz, Easy Ad, JDL, and Almighty KG. The first rap record by a non-rap group "King Tim III" is recorded by the Fatback Band. Sugarhill Gang's "Rapper's Delight" would go on to become the first known rap hit, reaching #36 on Billboard. Various obscure rap singles were also released: Grandmaster Flash & The Furious 5's "Super-rappin" and Spoonie Gee's "Spoonin' Rap" both on Enjoy Records, Kurtis Blow's "Christmas Rappin" on Mercury Records, and Jimmy Spicer's 13-minute long storytelling track "Adventures of Super Rhymes" on Dazz Records. Mr. Magic's 'Rap Attack' becomes the first hip-hop radio show on WHBI.

1980:
Afrika Bambaata and the Zulu Nation release their first 12" called Zulu Nation Throwdown Pt. 1 on Paul Winley Records. Kurtis Blow, the first rapper to appear on national television (Soul Train), releases "The Breaks" on Mercury Records. The record goes on to sell more than a million copies. Hip-hop gradually evolves into big business. After meeting Fab 5 Freddy and others, Blonde releases "Rapture" featuring rap vocals by lead singer Debbie Harry.

1981:
Grandmaster Flash releases "The Adventures of Grand Master Flash on the Wheels of Steel," the first record to ultimately capture the sounds of live DJ scratching on

wax. On February 14th, The Funky 4 plus One More perform their classic hit, "That's The Joint" on NBC's Saturday Night Live becoming the first hip hop group to appear on national television. The Beastie Boys are formed. The group consists of Adam Horovitz (King Ad-Rock), Adam Yauch (MCA), Michael Diamon (Mike D).

1982:
Afrika Bambaataa and the Soul Sonic Force release the techno-heavy "Planet Rock" on Tommy Boy Records. The record samples portions of Kraftwerk's "Trans-Europe Express." Grandmaster Flash & the Furious 5 release "The Message" on Sugarhill Records. Kool Moe Dee humiliates Busy Bee in a spontaneous rap battle. Since then, emcee battling has become an inseparable part of Hip-Hop. Fab 5 Freddy and Charlie Ahearn co-produce Wild Style, a hip-hop film featuring Cold Crush Brothers, Grandmaster Flash, Grandwizard Theodore, DJ AJ, Grandmixer D.S.T, graf writers Lee, Zephyr, Fab 5 Freddy, Lady Pink, Crash, Daze, Dondi, and members of the Rock Steady Crew. Wild Style has since inspired several other hip-hop-themed movies.

1983:
Ice T helps pioneer gangsta rap in the west coast with his rapcore singles "Body Rock" and "Killers." Grand Master Flash and Melle Mel (Furious 5) record the anti-cocaine single "White Lines (Don't Do It)," which

becomes a rap hit. Grandmaster Flash later sues Sugarhill Records for $5 million in royalties. The dispute causes the group to break up, signaling the looming danger of corporate control in hip-hop. Run DMC releases "It's Like That" b/w "Sucker MC's."

1984:
Russell Simmons and Rick Rubin team up to launch one of the most important record labels ever, Def Jam Records. Def Jam releases its first record, "It's Yours" by T La Rock, followed by LL Cool J's "I Need A Beat." Hip-Hop discovers that touring is a great way to generate income, as the Fresh Fest concert featuring Whodini, Kurtis Blow, Fat Boys, and Run DMC, reels in $3.5 million for 27 dates. Battle rap assumes the spotlight in hip-hop, as UTFO's "Roxanne Roxanne" diss song attracts over 100 responses. The most popular response came from a 14-year old female named Roxanne Shante. Shante's "Roxanne's Revenge" allegedly recorded in Marley Marl's living room sold more than 250,000 copies. Dougie Fresh (aka The Entertainer) releases The Original Human Beat Box(Vindertainment Records). Michael Jackson does 'the moonwalk' at the Grammys, borrowing b-boy dance elements from LA breakers.

1985:
Sugarhill Records goes into bankruptcy and is forced out

of business. Salt 'n' Pepa make their first appearance on Super Nature's "The Show Stopper."

1986:
The Beastie Boys release Licensed To Ill on Def Jam (executive-produced by Rick Rubin).
James Smith, a native of Houston, Texas, assembles The Geto Boys. The original lineup consisted of MCs Raheim, Jukebox, DJ Ready Red, and Sir Rap-A-Lot. The group also featured Little Billy, a dancing dwarf who later picked up the microphone as Bushwick Bill. Following a short break-up in 1988, Smith invited local emcee Willie D and multi-instrumentalist Akshun (later known as Scarface) to complete the lineup. The Geto Boys (now made up of Scarface, Willie D, and Bushwick Bill) was a driving force in the evolution of southern rap.

1987:
Following the release of Boogie Down Productions' Criminal Minded LP, Scott LaRock is shot and killed in the South Bronx while attempting to settle a dispute. Public Enemy stuns the world with their introductory album, Yo! Bum Rush The Show, signaling the genesis of politically-charged Hip-Hop. The original members of the group include Chuck D (Carlton Ridenhour), Flavor Flav (William Drayton), Professor Griff (Richard Griffin), and DJ Terminator X (Norman Rogers).

1988:
After years of being neglected by the mainstream media, hip-hop gets its own show on MTV, "Yo! MTV Raps." N.W.A pioneers the gangsta rap movement with their gold album, Straight Outta Compton. Def Jam founders Russell Simmons and Rick Rubin part ways; Simmons opts for distribution through CBS/Columbia Records, while Rubin goes on to found Def American. Landmark album releases: Ultramagnetic MC's – Critical Breakdown, and Big Daddy Kane – Long Live The Kane.

1989:
After a life-long battle with crack addiction, Cowboy, a member of Grandmaster Flash's Furious 5 dies at the age of 28. A group of high school friends join the Native Tongues as promoters of the Afrocentricity Movement to make African-Americans aware of their heritage.
These Manhattan-based friends would later form A Tribe Called Quest (Q-Tip, Ali Shaheed Muhammad, Phife Dawg, and Jarobi). A Dallas-based protégé of Dr. Dre known as D.O.C releases No One Can Do It Better. While the album was making rounds on the charts, D.O.C. found himself in a severe car crash. While D.O.C. survived the accident, his vocal career didn't and started songwriting.

1990:

2 Pac joins Digital Underground as a dancer and a roadie.

The "Stretch & Bobbito Show" is launched. Both a Florida record store owner and Luther Campbell are arrested over 2 Live Crew's controversial album, As Nasty as They Wanna Be.

MC Hammer hit mainstream success with the multi platinum album Please Hammer, Don't Hurt 'Em. The record reached and the first single, "Can't Touch This" charted on the top ten of the billboard hot 100. MC Hammer became one of the most successful rappers of the early nineties and one of the first household names in the genre. The album raised rap music to a new level of popularity. It was the first Hip-Hop album certified diamond by the RIAA for sales of over ten million. It remains one of the genre's all-time best-selling albums. To date, the album has sold as many as 18 million units.

1991:
N.W.A's sophomore album N****z For Life sells over 954,000 copies in its first week of release, reaching #1 on the pop charts. The album paves way for many more hardcore rap albums that would follow. Busta Rhymes appears on A Tribe Called Quest's "Scenario." Cypress Hill (B-Real, DJ Muggs, and Sen Dog) release their self-titled debut, and initiate a campaign to legalize hemp. The Notorious B.I.G. is featured in the "Unsigned Hype" column of The Source magazine.

1992:

The police beating of Rodney King. Dr. Dre released The Chronic. As well as helping to establish West Coast gangsta rap as more commercially viable than East Coast hip hop, this album founded a style called G Funk, which soon came to dominate West Coast hip Hop. The style was further developed and popularized by Snoop Dogg's 1993's album "Doggystyle". The Wu-Tang Clan shot to fame around the same time. Being from New York City's Staten Island, the Wu-Tang Clan brought the East Coast back into the mainstream at a time when the West Coast mainly dominated rap. Other major artists in the so-called East Coast hip hop renaissance included The Notorious B.I.G., Jay-Z, and Nas. The Beastie Boys continued their success throughout the decade crossing color lines and gaining respect from many different artists.

Record labels based out of Atlanta, St. Louis, and New Orleans gained fame for their local scenes. The midwest rap scene was also notable, with the fast vocal styles from artists such as Bone Thugs-n-Harmony, and Twista. By the end of the decade, hip hop was an integral part of popular music, and many American pop songs had hip Hop components.

1993:

A Tribe Called Quest release their third album, Midnight Marauders, featuring a who-is-who-in-Hip-Hop album cover. Dr. Dre's The Chronic attains multi-platinum status. Wu-Tang Clan release 36 Chambers. The line-up consists of Prince Rakeem (The RZA), Raekwon, Ol' Dirty Bastard, Method Man, Ghostface Killah, Genius (GZA), U-God, Master Killa and Inspectah Deck. Mobb Deep (Prodigy and Havoc) release their debut LP, Juvenile Hell.

1994:

Nas' first entry, Illmatic goes gold and is widely received as one of the greatest hip-hop albums ever. Common releases Resurrection and is lauded as an intelligent lyricist. Warren G's Regulate: The G-Funk Era is certified 4x platinum. 2 Pac is robbed and shot 5 times in a New York recording studio. He recovers from the shooting. Pac is later sentenced to 8 months in prison.

1995:

Queen Latifah wins a Grammy award in the "Best Rap Solo Performance" category for her hit "Unity." 2 Pac signs a deal with Death Row Records after Suge Knight posts a $1.4 million bail.
Eric Wright (Eazy-E of N.W.A) dies of AIDS on March 20th at the age of 31.

1996:

The Score, a fusion of conscious lyrics with reggae-tinged soulsonics, becomes The Fugees' biggest album. The album debuts at No.1 and grabs two Grammys, thus, breathing a new life into socially aware Hip-Hop. The

Music of Black Origin (MOBO) Awards are launched in the U.K. The Fugees walk away with two trophies. Jay-Z drops his highly-lauded debut, Reasonable Doubt. His "charismatic rapper" approach would later spawn throngs of emulators.

24-year old Snoop Dogg and his bodyguard McKinley Lee are acquitted of the murder of Philip Woldemariam, a 20-year-old Ethiopian immigrant gunned down in August 1993. On September 7th, Tupac Shakur is fatally wounded after sustaining multiple gunshots as he rode in a car driven by Death Row Records CEO Marion "Suge" Knight near the Las Vegas strip. Tupac died 5 days later. His death rekindled the debate on whether rap promotes violence or just reflects the ugly side of the streets.

1997:
The Notorious B.I.G. (born Christopher Wallace), is shot and killed March 9, after a party at the Petersen Automotive Museum in Los Angeles. Like Pac's murder, Biggie's death is still an unsolved mystery. Missy Misdemeanor Elliott redefines hip-hop and R & B with her first album, Supa Dupa Fly. Having broken barriers as a successful female producer, Missy would go on to become the highest selling female rapper of all time. Parent company Interscope Records sells its interest in Death Row Records and severs ties with the label. Chicago MC Juice defeats Eminem on his way to winning the year's Scribble Jam competition. (Scribble Jam is the

largest showcase of underground hip-hop in the United States.) Roc-A-Fella sells a 50 percent stake to Island Def Jam for $1.5 million.

1998:
Dr. Dre inks Eminem to his Aftermath imprint. Lauryn Hill's solo debut, The Miseducation of Lauryn Hill, scores her 11 Grammy nominations and 5 wins, including Album of the Year and Best New Artist. "Hard Knock Life (Ghetto Anthem)" marks the beginning of Jay-Z's mainstream breakthrough and helps move 5 million units of Vol 2: Hardknock Life. The chorus is sampled from the Broadway play "Annie." Shyne (born Jamal Barrow) signs a lucrative record deal with Diddy's Bad Boy Entertainment.

1999:
Backed by producer Dr. Dre, Eminem zooms past racial hurdles and sells 4 million copies of his debut, The Slim Shady LP. Production duo The Neptunes (Chad Hugo & Pharrell Williams) dominate the airwave with a string of radio hits, including Kelis' "Caught Out There," ODB's "Got Your Money," Noreaga's "Oh No," and Mase's "One Big Fiesta." Their infectious, bling-tinged sound would later become an unofficial requisite on hip-hop albums. Dr. Dre puts the west coast back on the spotlight with his comeback LP 2001.

2000:

Dr. Dre files a lawsuit against MP3-swapping firm Napster. Congresswoman Cynthia McKinney holds the first Hip-Hop Powershop summit to address the various political, economic, and social issues affecting the youth. DJ Craze wins the Technics DMC World DJ Championship 3 consecutive times. Eminem, through the release of his well received second album Marshall Mathers LP, solidifies his place as rap's future great. The title sells 1.76-million copies in its first week and later scores two Grammys for the rapper.

MOMENTS IN POP CULTURE HISTORY

In the entire brief history of rap music, a few moments have gone—as the saying goes—deeper than rap.

These are not the scenes and headlines that made hip-hop "relevant" as much as the moments where Hip-Hop characters, ideals, and narratives ended up on the front pages of national papers, shifting the American news cycle and making the sounds, lyrics, and faces of the genre as much a story as any great world leader or event. Sometimes, like Bill Clinton calling out Sister Souljah, the moments were gasoline on fire. Other times, they were just a spark on a fuse waiting to be lit, like Dr. Dre making headphones everybody's most essential personal style accessory.

These are moments of protest, of struggle, and of shame. These are moments of pride and of power. These are moments that define the music we so often take for granted, whether it's Kanye saying some shit about an American President, or an American President saying some shit about Kanye—and then campaigning with Jay-Z not long after. From the subliminal moments to the most pronounced, from the film and TV show moments to the moments when the corridors of political power were forced to confront rappers—yes, rappers—these are those times when Hip-Hop splashed into the mainstream, by all means necessary.

Hip-Hop's taken everything from figurative bows thrown to literal shots fired. Yet, they weren't game changers for rap so much as for pop culture, moments of pure, uncut recognition that this isn't just a subculture, or a trend, but pieces of the greater American mosaic. From Kanye to Clinton, from Style Wars to who Wu-Tang's for, these are the 40 Biggest Hip-Hop Moments in Pop Culture History.

The Moment: What happens when a punk band trying to spice up its repertoire attempts to do so by adopting what New York City punk bands—let alone pop culture—rarely ventured to for its hits? You get the first rap video on MTV, in MTV's first month on the air, in their first 90-video rotation, which arrived in the form of Blondie's "Rapture," the entire coda of which is rapped by Debbie Harry. To hammer the point home, Blondie also recruited hip-hop luminaries to appear in the video with them, like Fab Five Freddy (who's name-checked in the song), Lee Quinones, and Jean-Michel Basquiat.

The Impact: "Rapture" came at a weirdly perfect time as it wasn't just the first video featuring rap on MTV but was a video in MTV's first real "rotation," where it stayed for a few months. In other words, eyes from all over the country saw this young white woman doing the "hip-hop" thing.

The Upshot: At the time, it was neither an abomination nor a momentous occasion, but just a weird rock thing that was, if not amusing, then actually fairly cool. The video helped cement Blondie's place as one of the more progressive bands in contemporary rock, and set the precedent for rock embracing hip-hop (and vice-versa).

The Moment: At the beginning of the new decade, Newsweek—then one of two magazines in every other suburban, middle-class household, along with Time—released a cover about the anger of rap music. The editors wanted to choose between two rap acts: LL Cool J, and Tone Loc. They went with Loc.

The Impact: Tone Loc didn't become much "harder" of a rapper than he already "was." The impact on Loc's career was minimal at best. The cover's effect on perceptions of rap, however, wasn't insignificant. To one segment of America, it was a sign of things to come: Rap and these rappers are scary, it screamed, so you better lock away your children. To another segment of America, it screamed: People who write newsweeklies know nothing about rap, as evidenced by their selection of Tone Loc to represent anger in rap.

The Upshot: To another, much smaller segment of America, it screamed: Wow, scaring people with rap is pretty compelling. Let's replicate it! And thus, thousands of fear-based pieces about the dangers of angry rappers were born, in a tradition that continues to this day. Meanwhile, Loc went on to have one of the most family-friendly careers in acting as a rapper has ever had, including famously being talked to by the ass of Jim Carrey in Ace Ventura: Pet Detective.

The Moment: Other stations had played rap before KDAY, but it wasn't until the hiring of Greg "Mack" Macmillan as their program director and afternoon host that everything changed. Mack turned the station into a Hip-Hop powerhouse, recruiting young talent to not only to DJ, but to have their ears to the streets. One such talent pool? The World Class Wreckin' Cru, whose Dr. Dre had started to mix tracks together on a mixer in real time, splicing old tracks into contemporary rap records.

The Impact: The station became one of the most influential outlets for rap nearly overnight, and broke some of the most important records in the history of rap. Moreover, it created the market for rap radio formats, and if hot rap singles begin anywhere, it's on rap format radio.

The Upshot: KDAY would eventually turn over from a rap format station in 1991, and would relaunch as a less-influential version of the original in 2004 as a middle-ground urban contemporary station. More importantly, however, KDAY lead terrestrial radio executives to realize that the rap format would be a crucial one in years to come, spawning the creation of rap radio all over America.

The Moment: Stand-up comedy—great, edgy, stand-up comedy—was still too hot for most televised broadcasts, let alone stand-up by black comedians, who had to overcome major networks' worries about audience pull and standards and practices troubles. Enter Def Jam founder and label head Russell Simmons, who found himself with a production deal at HBO, that cable channel you had to pay extra for, with all the movies, and a few of its own TV shows that you couldn't find anywhere else. Slapping his record label's name on a late-night stand-up hour on pay cable, Simmons found a place to infuse comedians' personas and performances with a hip-hop aesthetic, and create a home for unabated humor that was topical for a segment of the population that had long gone without one. In doing so, Def Comedy Jam was born.

The Impact: While protested by some for what was

perceived as offensive content that reinforced negative black stereotypes, the show would go on to receive relatively high marks from TV critics.

The Upshot: Def Comedy Jam not only paved the way for edgy stand-up comedy on television, but cemented HBO's place in the media world as an outlet for edgier entertainment, period. It also furthered Russell Simmons' status as an entrepreneur of hip-hop outside of the realm of music and gave rise to a host (Martin Lawrence) who went on to a wildly successful career of his own.

The Moment: Academy Award-nominee and Hollywood royalty actor Warren Beatty writes, produces, consults with Suge Knight on, and directs a movie about a California Senator who goes off the rails, beginning to speak his mind and truth to his own power, in the form of cringe-inducing raps, with an all-star rap soundtrack released by Interscope.

The Impact: Like the titular character, the movie was initially seen as a curious and naive attempt by old white Hollywood to reach out to young urban America, both by Beatty's Hollywood peers and casual viewers alike. As it turned out, both parties ended up loving it: Critics gave it generally positive reviews, the soundtrack produced one of the bigger hits of that summer (in the form of Pras, ODB, and Mya's "Ghetto Supastar"), and the unlikely cultural crossover actually, oddly, managed to work out.

The Upshot: While it hasn't aged so well and still can lay claim to one of the most universally reviled endings in '90s movie history, the film grossed $29 million worldwide, and picked up a handful of nominations for Beatty and Jeremy Pikser's screenplay (which only won a minor L.A. critics award, losing out almost universally to Shakespeare in Love or The Truman Show). The soundtrack was certified platinum by the RIAA. The movie was one of Warren Beatty's last great works, as he continues to ease off major projects.

The Moment: MTV rolled out one of the most unlikely pairings in the network's history to present the 1997 VMA for Best Dance Video: Martha Stewart and Busta Rhymes, introduced by Chris Rock as "one [who] knows how to make a really mean pot roast, and the other one is always roasted on pot." Martha showed up in muted browns, looking demure. Busta showed up in a red and gold kimono. "What the dilly, yo?" Busta grinned, as Martha Stewart looked both completely uncomfortable and also massively charmed. Martha talked about dropping some beats—or beets—and Busta shouted out Wu-Tang Clan and the Flipmode Squad. The entire thing was, in a word, surreal.

The Impact: It contributed to part a great year for both music videos and the Chris Rock-hosted MTV VMAs, which got high marks from TV and music critics as a high point in the brief history of the network and its awards ceremonies, and more crucially, MTV found itself encouraged to take bigger risks with pairings like Busta and Martha, especially after 1998's Ben Stiller-hosted VMAs failed to thrill in quite the same way. Enter the '99 VMAs, which were hosted again by Chris Rock, but this time, at the Met Opera, and had more than a few watercooler moments, like pairing the mothers of the Notorious B.I.G. and Tupac, or Lil' Kim and Diana Ross, who would jiggle Kim's pasty-covered breast on the VMA stage.

The Upshot: If, in 1997, you were asked who would spend more time in jail over the next fifteen years, you'd probably get this answer wrong. Busta Rhymes remained one of rap's most popular and eccentric acts, and then got very, very in shape, and stopped wearing kimonos, and ceased being weird (and wonderful, to an extent). He never did hard time. Martha Stewart continued to grow her media and kitchenware empire but did end up going to jail for insider trading. The VMAs fell into decline after the early Aughts, and have yet to reach quite the peak levels of excitement they generated in the late '90s.

The Moment: In 1985, as the holiday shopping season kicked into full gear, commercials for Swatch started appearing in New York City, featuring an unlikely celebrity endorsement: the Fat Boys, performing the song they'd recorded for the occasion, "Swatch Watch Presents A Merry Christmas."

The Impact: After a Swatch-sponsored tour with Run-DMC, Kurtis Blow, and Whodini, the endorsement of the watch-slingers—made possible by the Fat Boys' manager Charlie Stettler, a Swiss national—became one of the most successful cool-kid ad campaigns of all time, and shot the Fat Boys into the forefront of Hip-Hop as one of its most charismatic, charming, and irresistible acts.

The Upshot: The Fat Boys continued to appear in movies and TV shows (Disorderlies, an episode of "Miami Vice") and made some classic records along the way. More importantly, they proved that rappers were as capable of being a celebrity spokesperson as any other stripe, and thus, paved the way for so many of the multi-million dollar deals we know all too well to come.

The Moment: In the Spring of '97, a commercial starts to air for the Gap, featuring a new kind of spokesperson for the mall-sHopping standard of America: LL Cool J. In the spot, LL sports the Gap neck-to-toe. On his head, however, was a hat by a then little-known streetwear brand called FUBU, which stood for "For Us, By Us," given a shout by LL in the lyrics of his rap during the commercial, with those exact words.

The Impact: Executives for The Gap were supposedly furious, once they actually realized what had happened.

And here's what happened: FUBU's founder, Daymond John—an old friend of LL's from Hollis, Queens—kept pestering LL Cool J to wear his new clothing line, until LL actually did...to a shoot for his big Gap commerical. Orders for the clothing line exploded, and FUBU became the original monolithic rapper-endorsed streetwear brand, with revenues totaling somewhere around the $300 million mark in 1998.

TERMINOLOGY

Hip Hop music is a musical genre that developed as part of hip hop culture, and is defined by four key stylistic elements - Rapping, DJing/scratching, sampling (or synthesis), and beatboxing. Hip-hop began in the South Bronx of New York City in the 1970s. The term rap is often used synonymously with hip hop, but hip hop also denotes the practices of an entire subculture.

Rapping, also referred to as MCing or emceeing, is a vocal style in which the artist speaks lyrically, in rhyme and verse, generally to an instrumental or synthesized beat. Beats, almost always in 4/4 time signature, can be created by sampling and/or sequencing portions of other songs by a producer. They also incorporate synthesizers, drum machines, and live bands. Rappers may write, memorize, or improvise their lyrics and perform their works a cappella or to a beat.

THE TERM: HIP-HOP

Creation of the term hip hop is often credited to Keith Cowboy, rapper with Grandmaster Flash and the Furious Five. However, Lovebug Starski, Keith Cowboy, and DJ Hollywood used the term when the music was still known as disco rap. It is believed that Cowboy created the term while teasing a friend who had just joined the U.S. Army, by scat-singing the words "hip/Hop/hip/Hop" in a way that mimicked the rhythmic cadence of marching soldiers. Cowboy later worked the "Hip Hop" cadence into a part of his stage performance, which was quickly used by other artists such as The Sugarhill Gang in "Rapper's Delight".

Universal Zulu Nation founder, Afrika Bambaataa is credited first with using the term to describe the subculture in which the music belonged; although it is also suggested that it was a derogatory term to describe the type of music.

The first use of the term in print was in The Village Voice, by Steven Hager, later author of "A 1984 history of Hip Hop."

SEVENTIES' ROOTS OF HIP-HOP

The roots of hip hop are found in earlier African-American genres of music and traces as far back as pre-colonial Africa. The griots of West Africa are a group of traveling singers and poets who are part of an oral tradition dating back hundreds of years. Their vocal style is similar to that of rappers. The African-American traditions of signifyin', the dozens, and jazz poetry are all descended from the griots. In addition, musical 'comedy' acts such as Rudy Ray Moore and Blowfly are considered by some to be the forefathers of rap.

Within New York City, griot-like performances of spoken-word poetry and music by artists such as The Last Poets, Gil Scott-Heron and Jalal Mansur Nuriddin had a significant impact on the post-civil rights era culture of the 1960s and 1970s.

Hip Hop arose during the 1970s when block parties

became increasingly popular in New York City, particularly in the Bronx, where African American and Puerto Rican influences combined. Block parties incorporated DJs who played popular genres of music, especially funk and soul music. Due to the positive reception, DJs began isolating the percussion breaks of popular songs. This technique was then common in Jamaican dub music and had spread to New York City via the substantial Jamaican immigrant community. One of the first DJs in New York to use dub style mixing was the Jamaican-born DJ Kool Herc, who emigrated to the United States in 1967. Dub music had become popular in Jamaica due to the influence of American sailors and rhythm & blues. Large sound systems were set up to accommodate poor Jamaicans who couldn't afford to buy records and dub developed at the sound systems. Because the New York audience did not particularly like dub or reggae, Herc switched to using funk, soul and disco records. As the percussive breaks were generally short, Herc and other DJs began extending them using an audio mixer and two records.

Turntablist techniques, such as scratching (seemingly invented by Grand Wizzard Theodore, beat mixing/matching, and beat juggling eventually developed along with the breaks, creating a base that could be rapped over. These same techniques contributed to the popularization of remixes as the looping, sampling and remixing of another's music, often without the original artist's knowledge or consent, can be seen as an evolution of Jamaican dub music, and would become a hallmark of the hip hop style. Jamaican immigrants also provided an influence on the vocal style of rapping by delivering simple raps at their parties, inspired by the Jamaican tradition of toasting. DJs and MCs would often add call and response chants, often consisting of a basic chorus, to allow the performer to gather his thoughts (e.g. "one, two, three, y'all, to the beat").

Later, the MCs grew more varied in their vocal and rhythmic delivery, incorporating brief rhymes, often with a sexual or scatological theme, in an effort to differentiate themselves and to entertain the audience. These early raps incorporated the dozens, a product of African American culture. Kool Herc & the Herculoids were the first Hip Hop group to gain recognition in New York citation needed, but the number of MC teams increased over time.

Often these were collaborations between former gangs, such as Afrikaa Bambaataa's Universal Zulu Nation - now an international organization. Melle Mel, a rapper with The Furious Five is often credited with being the first rap lyricist to call himself an "MC." During the early 1970s B-boying arose during block parties, as b-boys and b-girls got in front of the audience to dance in a distinctive and frenetic style. The style was documented for release to a world wide audience for the first time in documentaries and movies such as Style Wars, Wild

Style, and Beat Street. The term "B-boy" was coined by DJ Kool Herc to describe the people who would wait for the break section of the song, getting in front of the audience to dance in a distinctive, frenetic style.

Although there were many early MCs that recorded solo projects of note, such as DJ Hollywood, Kurtis Blow and Spoonie Gee, the frequency of solo artists didn't increase until later with the rise of soloists with stage presence and drama, such as LL Cool J. Most early hip hop was dominated by groups where collaboration between the members was integral to the show. An example would be the early hip Hop group Funky Four Plus One, who performed in such a manner on Saturday Night Live in 1981. Hip Hop music was an outlet and a "voice" for the disenfranchised youth of low-economic areas as the culture reflected the social, economic and political realities of their lives.

INFLUENCE OF DISCO

Hip Hop music was influenced by disco and there was a backlash against it from its fans. According to Kurtis Blow, the early days of hip Hop were characterized by divisions between fans and detractors of disco music. Hip Hop had largely emerged as "a direct response to the watered down, Europeanised, disco music that permeated the airwaves", and the earliest hip hop was mainly based on hard funk loops. However, by 1979, disco instrumental loops/tracks had become the basis of much hip hop. The genre got the name, "disco rap". Ironically, Hip Hop was also a proponent in the eventual decline in disco's popularity.

DJ Pete Jones, Eddie Cheeba, DJ Hollywood, and Love Bug Starski were disco-influenced hip hop DJs. Their styles differed from other hip hop musicians who focused on rapid-fire rhymes and more complex rhythmic schemes. Afrika Bambaataa, Paul Winley, Grandmaster Flash, and Bobby Robinson were all members of this latter group.

In Washington, D.C. go-go emerged as a reaction against disco and eventually incorporated characteristics of Hip Hop during the early 1980s. The genre of electronic music behaved similarly, eventually evolving into what is known as House Music in Chicago and Techno in New York. (Read my book: House Rules: Dance with Me on this subject.)

TRANSITION TO RECORDING

The first hip hop recording is widely regarded to be The Sugarhill Gang's "Rapper's Delight", from 1979. However, much controversy surrounds this allegation as some regard "King Tim III (Personality Jock)" by The Fatback Band, which was released a few weeks before "Rapper's Delight", as a rap record. There are various other claimants for the title of first hip Hop record.

By the early 1980s, all the major elements and techniques of the Hip Hop genre were in place. Though not yet mainstream, hip hop had permeated outside of New York City; it could be found in cities as diverse as Atlanta, Los Angeles, Washington, D.C., Baltimore, Dallas, Kansas City, San Antonio, Miami, Seattle, St. Louis, New Orleans, Houston, and Toronto. Indeed, "Funk You Up" (1979), the first Hip Hop record released by a female group, and the second single released by

Sugar Hill Records, was performed by The Sequence, a group from Columbia, South Carolina which featured Angie Stone.

Despite the genre's growing popularity, Philadelphia was, for many years, the only city whose contributions could be compared to New York City's. Hip hop music became popular in Philadelphia in the late 1970s. The first released record was titled "Rhythm Talk", by Jocko Henderson.

The New York Times had dubbed Philadelphia the "Graffiti Capital of the World" in 1971. Philadelphia native DJ Lady B recorded "To the Beat Y'All" in 1979, and became the first female solo hip hop artist to record music. Schoolly D, starting in 1984 and also from Philadelphia, began creating a style that would later be known as gangsta rap.

The 1980s marked the diversification of Hip Hop as the genre developed more complex styles. Early examples of the diversification process can be identified through such tracks as Grandmaster Flash's "The Adventures of Grandmaster Flash on the Wheels of Steel" (1981), a single consisting entirely of sampled tracks as well as Afrika Bambaataa's "Planet Rock" (1982), which signified the fusion of hip Hop music with electro. In addition, Rammellzee & K-Rob's "Beat Bop" (1983) was a 'slow jam' which had a dub influence with its use of reverb and echo as texture and playful sound effects. The mid-

1980s was marked by the influence of rock music, with the release of such albums as King of Rock and Licensed to Ill.

Heavy usage of the new generation of drum machines such as the Oberheim DMX and Roland 808 models was a characteristic of many 1980s songs. To this day, the 808-kickdrum is traditionally used by hip hop producers. Over time sampling technology became more advanced; however, earlier producers such as Marley Marl used drum machines to construct their beats from small excerpts of other beats in synchronisation, in his case, triggering 3 Korg sampling-delay units through a 808. Later, samplers such as the E-mu SP-1200 allowed not only more memory but more flexibility for creative production. This allowed the filtration and layering different hits, and with a possibility of re-sequencing them into a single piece.

With the emergence of a new generation of samplers such as the AKAI S900 in the late 1980s, producers did not require the aid of tape loops. Public Enemy's first album was created with the help of large tape loops. The process of looping break into a breakbeat now became more common with a sampler, now doing the job which so far had been done manually by the DJ. In 1989, DJ Mark James under the moniker "45 King", released "The 900 Number", a breakbeat track created by synchronizing samplers and vinyl.

The lyrical content of hip hop evolved as well. The early styles presented in the 1970s soon were replaced with metaphorical lyrics over more complex, multi-layered instrumentals. Artists such as Melle Mel, Rakim, Chuck D, and KRS-One revolutionized hip Hop by transforming it into a more mature art form. The influential single "The Message" (1982) by Grandmaster Flash and the Furious Five is widely considered to be the pioneering force for conscious rap.

During the early 1980s, electro music was fused with elements of the hip hop movement, largely led by artists such as Cybotron, Hashim, Planet Patrol and Newcleus. The most notable proponent was Afrika Bambaataa who produced the single "Planet Rock".

Some rappers eventually became mainstream pop performers. Kurtis Blow's appearance in a Sprite commercial marked the first hip Hop musician to represent a major product. The 1981 song "Christmas Wrapping" by the new-wave band The Waitresses was one of the first pop songs to use some rapping in the delivery.

NATIONALIZATION & INTERNATIONALIZATION

Prior to the 1980s, rap music was largely confined within the context of the United States. However, during the 1980s, it began its spread and became a part of the music scene in dozens of countries. In the early part of the decade, B-boying became the first aspect of hip hop culture to reachGermany, Japan, Australia and South Africa, where the crew Black Noise established the practice before beginning to rap later in the decade. Musician and presenter Sidney became France's first black TV presenter with his show H.I.P. H.O.P. which screened on TF1 during 1984, a first for the genre worldwide. Radio Nova helped launch other French stars including Dee Nasty whose 1984 album Paname City Rappin' along with compilations Rapattitude 1 and 2 contributed to a general awareness of Hip Hop in France.

Hip Hop has always kept a very close relationship with

the Latino community in New York. DJ Disco Wiz and the Rock Steady Crew were among early innovators from Puerto Rico. combining English and Spanish in the lyrics. The Mean Machine recorded their first song under the label "Disco Dreams" in 1981, while Kid Frost from Los Angeles began his career in 1982.

Cypress Hill was formed in 1988 in the suburb of South Gate outside Los Angeles when Senen Reyes (born in Havana) and his younger brother Ulpiano Sergio (Mellow Man Ace) moved from Cuba to South Gate with his family in 1971. They teamed up with DVX from Queens (New York), Lawrence Muggerud (DJ Muggs) and Louis Freese (B-Real), a Mexican/Cuban-American native of Los Angeles. After the departure of "Ace" to begin his solo career the group adopted the name of Cypress Hill named after a street running through a neighborhood nearby in South Los Angeles.

Hip hop in Japan is said to have begun when Hiroshi Fujiwara returned to Japan and started playing Hip-Hop records in the early 1980s. The Japanese genre tends to be most directly influenced by America's old school, taking from the era's catchy beats, dance culture, while adding a carefree approach in incorporating it into their own. As a result, Hip Hop stands as one of the most commercially viable mainstream music genres in Japan, and the line between it and pop music is frequently blurred.

EARLY NEW SCHOOL

The new school of Hip Hop was the second wave of hip hop music, originating in 1983–84 with the early records of Run-D.M.C. and LL Cool J. As with the hip hop preceding it, the new school came predominately from New York City. The new school was initially characterized in form by drum machine-led minimalism, with influences from rock music. It was notable for taunts and boasts about rapping, and socio-political commentary, both delivered in an aggressive, self-assertive style. I

n image as in song, its artists projected a tough, cool, street b-boy attitude. These elements contrasted sharply with the funk and disco influenced outfits, novelty hits, live bands, synthesizers and party rhymes of artists prevalent prior to 1984, and rendered them old-school. New school artists made shorter songs that could more easily gain radio play, and more cohesive LPs than their old school counterparts.

By 1986, their releases began to establish the Hip Hop album as a fixture of the mainstream. Hip Hop music became commercially successful, as exemplified by the Beastie Boys' 1986 album, "Licensed to Ill," which was the first rap album to hit the Billboard charts.

THE GOLDEN AGE

Hip Hop's "golden age" (or "golden era") is a name given to a period in mainstream Hip Hop—usually cited as between the mid 1980s and the mid 1990s—said to be characterized by its diversity, quality, innovation and influence. There were strong themes of Afrocentricity and political militancy, while the music was experimental and the sampling, eclectic. There was often a strong jazz influence. The artists most often associated with the phrase are Public Enemy, Boogie Down Productions, Eric B. & Rakim, De La Soul, A Tribe Called Quest, Gang Starr, Big Daddy Kane and the Jungle Brothers.

The golden age is noted for its innovation – a time "when it seemed that every new single reinvented the genre" according to Rolling Stone. Referring to "hip-hop in its golden age", Spin's editor-in-chief Sia Michel says, "there were so many important, groundbreaking albums coming out right about that time", and MTV's Sway Calloway adds: "The thing that made that era so great is that nothing was contrived. Everything was still being discovered and everything was still innovative and new". Writer William Jelani Cobb says "what made the era they inaugurated worthy of the term golden was the sheer number of stylistic innovations that came into existence... in these golden years, a critical mass of mic prodigies were literally creating themselves and their art form at the same time".

The specific time period that the golden age covers varies slightly from different sources. Some place it square in the 1980s and 1990s – Rolling Stone refers to "rap's '86-'99 golden age", and MSNBC states, "the "Golden Age" of Hip-Hop music: The '80s" and '90s".

GANGSTA RAP & WEST COAST

Gangsta rap is a subgenre of Hip-Hop that reflects the violent stories and lifestyles of inner-city youths. Gangsta is a non-rhotic pronunciation of the word "gangster." The genre was pioneered in the mid 1980s by rappers such as Schooly D and Ice T, and was popularized in the later part of the 1980s by groups like N.W.A. Ice-T released "6 in the Mornin'", which is often regarded as the first gangsta rap song, in 1986. After the national attention that Ice-T and N.W.A created in the late 1980s and early 1990s, gangsta rap became the most commercially lucrative subgenre of hip hop.

N.W.A is the group most frequently associated with pioneering gangsta rap. Their lyrics were more violent, openly confrontational, and shocking than those of established rap acts, featuring incessant profanity and, controversially, use of the word "nigger". These lyrics were placed over rough, rock guitar-driven beats, contributing to the music's hard-edged feel. The first blockbuster gangsta rap album was N.W.A's Straight Outta Compton, released in 1988. Straight Outta Compton would establish West Coast hip hop as a vital genre, and establish Los Angeles as a legitimate rival to hip hop's long-time capital, New York City. Straight Outta Compton sparked the first major controversy regarding hip hop lyrics when their song "Fuck Tha Police" earned a letter from FBI Assistant Director, Milt Ahlerich, strongly expressing law enforcement's resentment of the song. Due to the influence of Ice T and N.W.A, gangsta rap is often credited as being an originally West Coast phenomenon, despite the contributions of East Coast acts like Boogie Down Productions in shaping the genre.

The subject of gangsta rap has caused a great deal of controversy over the years. Criticism has come from both left and right-wing commentators, politicians and religious leaders. Gangsta rappers often find themselves defending their actions by saying that they are describing the reality of inner-city life, and that they are only adopting a character, like an actor playing a role, thus behaving in ways that they may not necessarily endorse.

WORLD HIP HOP

In Haiti, Hip-Hop was developed in the early 1980s, and is mostly accredited to Master Dji and his songs "Vakans" and "Politik Pam". What later became known as "Rap Kreyòl" grew in popularity in the late 1990s with King Posse and Original Rap Stuff. Due to cheaper recording technology and flows of equipment to Haiti, more Rap Kreyòl groups are recording songs, even after the January 12th earthquake.

In the Dominican Republic, a recording by Santi Y Sus Duendes and Lisa M became the first single of meren-rap, a fusion of Hip Hop and merengue.

New York City experienced a heavy Jamaican hip-hop influence during the 1990s. This influence was brought on by cultural shifts particularly because of the heightened immigration of Jamaicans to New York City and the American-born Jamaican youth who were coming of age during the 1990s. Rap artists such as De La Soul and Black Star have produced albums influenced by Jamaican roots.

In Europe, Africa, and Asia, Hip-Hop began to move from the underground to mainstream audiences and was the domain of both ethnic nationals and immigrants. British hip hop, for example, became a genre of its own and spawned many artists such as Wiley, Dizzee Rascal, The Streets and many more.

Germany produced the well-known "Die Fantastischen Vier" as well as several Turkish performers like the controversial Cartel, Kool Savaş, and Azad. Similarly,

France has produced a number of native-born stars, MC Solaar, Rohff, Rim'K or Booba. In the Netherlands, important nineties rappers include The Osdorp Posse, a crew from Amsterdam, Extince, from Oosterhout, and Postmen.

Italy found its own rappers, including Jovanotti and Articolo, grow nationally renowned, while the Polish scene began in earnest early in the decade with the rise of PM Cool Lee.

In Romania, B.U.G. Mafia came out of Bucharest's Pantelimon neighborhood, and their brand of gangsta rap underlines the parallels between life in Romania's Communist-era apartment blocks and in the housing projects of America's ghettos.

Israel and Palestinian Hip Hop grew greatly in popularity at the end of the decade, with several stars including Palestinian rapper (Tamer Nafer) and Israeli (Subliminal) hitting the scenes.

In Asia, mainstream stars rose to prominence in the Philippines, led by Francis Magalona, Rap Asia, MC Lara and Lady Diane. In Japan, where underground rappers had previously found a limited audience, and popular teen idols brought a style called J-rap to the top of the charts in the middle of the 1990s.

Latinos had played an integral role in the early development of hip hop, and the style had spread to parts of Latin America, such as Cuba, early in its history. In Mexico, popular hip hop began with the success of Calo [disambiguation needed] in the early 1990s. Later in the decade, with Hispanic rap groups like Cypress Hill gained fame on the American music charts while Mexican rap rock groups, such as Control Machete, rose to prominence in their country. An annual Cuban Hip Hop concert held at Alamar in Havana helped popularize Cuban hip hop, beginning in 1995. Hip Hop grew steadily more popular in Cuba, mainly because of official governmental support for all musicians.

The Brazilian hip hop scene is considered to be the second biggest in the world, just behind American hip Hop. It is heavily associated with racial and economic inequalities in the country, where a lot of blacks live in poverish situations in the violent slums, known in Brazil as favelas. São Paulo is where hip hop began in the country, but it soon spread all over Brazil, and today, almost every big Brazilian city, such as Rio de Janeiro, Salvador, Curitiba, Porto Alegre, Belo Horizonte, Recife and Brasilia, has a hip hop scene.

Racionais MC's, MV Bill, Marcelo D2, Rappin Hood, Jay Nano, Thaíde and Dj Hum, Bonde do Tigrão, Bonde do Rolê, GOG, RZO are considered the most powerful names in Brazilian hip hop music industry.

GLIMPSES OF WEST COAST HIP HOP

After N.W.A broke up, Dr. Dre released The Chronic in 1992, which peaked at #1 on the R&B/hip hop chart, on the pop chart and spawned a pop single with "Nuthin' but a "G" Thang." The Chronic took West Coast rap in a new direction, influenced strongly by P funk artists, melding sleazy funk beats with slowly drawled lyrics. This came to be known as G-funk and dominated mainstream hip Hop for several years through a roster of artists on Death Row Records, including Tupac Shakur, whose single "To Live & Die in LA" was a big hit, andSnoop Dogg, whose Doggystyle included the songs "What's My Name" and "Gin and Juice," both top ten hits.

Detached from this scene, were other artists such as Freestyle Fellowship, The Pharcyde as well as more underground artists such as the Solesides collective (DJ

Shadow and Blackalicious amongst others) Jurassic, Ugly Duckling (hip hop group), People Under the Stairs, The Alkaholiks, and earlier,Souls of Mischief represented a return to the roots of sampling and well-planned rhyme schemes. Also, the west coast has *avant-garde* Hip Hop label known as the Anticon, where artist such as Dose One, Sole (artist), and many others make experimental Hip Hop that goes beyond the status quo.

GLIMPSES OF EAST COAST HIP HOP

- In the early 1990s, East Coast hip hop was dominated by the Native Tongues posse which was loosely composed of De La Soul with producer Prince Paul, A Tribe Called Quest, The Jungle Brothers, as well as their loose affiliates - 3rd Bass, Main Source, and the less successful Black Sheep & KMD. Although originally a *"daisy age"* conception stressing the positive aspects of life, darker material (such as De La Soul's thought-provoking "Millie Pulled a Pistol on Santa") soon crept in.

- Artists such as Masta Ace (particularly for SlaughtaHouse) & Brand Nubian, Public Enemy, Organized Konfusion had a more overtly militant pose, both in sound and manner. Biz Markie, the "clown prince of hip hop", was causing himself and all other hip-hop producers a problem with his appropriation of the Gilbert O'Sullivan song "Alone again, naturally".

- In the mid-1990s, artists such as the Wu-Tang Clan, Nas and The Notorious B.I.G. increased New York's visibility at a time when hip hop was mostly dominated by West Coast artists. The mid to late 1990s saw a generation of rappers such as the members of D.I.T.C. such as the late Big L and Big Pun.

- The productions of RZA, particularly for Wu-Tang Clan, became influential with artists such as Mobb Deep due to the combination of somewhat detached instrumental loops, highly compressed and processed drums and gangsta lyrical content. Wu-Tang affiliate albums such as Raekwon the Chef's Only Built 4 Cuban Linx and GZA's Liquid Swords are now viewed as classics along with Wu-Tang "core" material.

- Producers such as DJ Premier (primarily for Gangstarr but also for other affiliated artists such as Jeru the Damaja), Pete Rock (With CL Smooth and supplying beats for many others), Buckwild, Large Professor, Diamond D and The 45 King supplying beats for numerous MCs regardless of location.

- Albums such as Nas's Illmatic, Jay-Z's Reasonable Doubt and O.C.'s Word...Life are made up of beats from this pool of producers.

- Later in the decade, the business acumen of the Bad

Boy Records tested itself against Jay-Z and his Roc-A-Fella Records and, on the West Coast, Death Row Records.

- The rivalry between the East Coast and the West Coast rappers eventually turned personal, aided in part by the music media.

- Although the "big business" end of the market dominated matters commercially the late 1990s to early 2000s saw a number of relatively successful East Coast indie labels such as Rawkus Records (with whom Mos Def gained great success) and later Def Jux; the history of the two labels is intertwined, the latter having been started by EL-P of Company Flow in reaction to the former, and offered an outlet for more underground artists such as Mike Ladd, Aesop Rock, Mr Lif, RJD2, Cage and Cannibal Ox. Other acts such as the Hispanic Arsonists and slam poet turned MC Saul Williams met with differing degrees of success.

DIVERSIFICATION OF STYLES

In the late 1990s, the styles of Hip Hop diversified. Southern rap became popular in the early 1990s, with the releases of Arrested Development's "3 Years, 5 Months & 2 Days in the Life Of... " in 1992, Goodie Mob's "Soul Food", in 1995 and OutKast's "ATLiens" in 1996. All three groups were from Atlanta, Georgia. Later, Master P (Ghetto D) built up a roster of artists (the No Limit posse) based out of New Orleans, Master P Incorporated. Rap groups with G-Funk and Miami bass along with other distinctive sounds from St. Louis, Chicago, Washington D.C., Detroit and other big cities gained popularity.

In the 1990s, elements of hip hop continued to be assimilated into other genres of popular music. Neo Soul, for example, combined hip hop and soul music.

In the 1980s and 1990s, rapcore, rap rock and rap metal,

fusions of hip hop and hardcore punk, rock and heavy metal became popular genres of rap music among mainstream audiences. Rage Against the Machine and Limp Bizkit were among the most well-known bands who played across these genres.

Digable Planets' 1993 release Reachin' (A New Refutation of Time and Space) was an influential jazz rap record sampling the likes of Don Cherry, Sonny Rollins, Art Blakey, Herbie Mann, Herbie Hancock, Grant Green, and Rahsaan Roland Kirk. It spawned the hit single "Rebirth of Slick (Cool Like Dat)" which reached 16 on the Billboard Hot 100.

White rappers like the Beastie Boys, House of Pain and 3rd Bass had had some popular success or critical acceptance from the Hip-Hop colored community, but Eminem's success, in 1999 with the platinum "The Slim Shady LP," surprised many in the ghettos.

The popularity of hip hop music continued through the 2000s. In the year 2000, "The Marshall Mathers LP" by Eminem sold over ten million copies in the United States and was the fastest-selling hip hop album of all time while Nelly's debut LP, "Country Grammar," sold over nine million. In the 2000s, crunk music, a derivative of Southern hip hop, gained considerable popularity via the likes of Lil Jon and the Ying Yang Twins.

Hip hop influences also found their way increasingly into mainstream pop during this period mainly the mid

2000s. In the East Coast, pop acts with hip-hop ventures grew tremendously.

The United States also saw the success of alternative hip hop from groups like The Roots, Dilated Peoples, Gnarls Barkley and Mos Def, who achieved significant recognition. Gnarls Barkley's album, "St. Elsewhere," which contained a fusion of funk, neo soul and hip hop, had debuted at number #20 on the Billboard 200 Chart.

ACROSS THE WORLD

The continuation of hip hop can also be seen in different national contexts. In Tanzania, maintained popular acts of their own in the early 2000s, infusing local styles of Afrobeat and arabesque melodies, dancehall and hip-hop beats, and Swahili lyrics. Scandinavian, especially Danish and Swedish, performers became well known outside of their country, while Hip Hop continued its spread into new regions, including Russia, Japan, Philippines, Canada, China, Korea, India and especially Vietnam. Of particular importance is the influence on East Asian nations, where hip hop music has become fused with local popular music to form different styles such as K-pop, C-pop and J-pop.

In the Netherlands, MC Brainpower went from being an underground battle rapper to mainstream recognition in the Benelux, thus influencing numerous rap artists in the region. In Israel, rapper Subliminal reaches out to Israeli youth with political and religious-themed lyrics, usually with a Zionist message. One of the countries outside the US where Hip-Hop is most popular is the United Kingdom. In the 2000s a derivative genre from Hip-Hop (as well as UK Garage and Drum and Bass) known as Grime became popular with artists such as Dizzee Rascal becoming successful. Although it is immensely popular, many British politicians criticize the music for what they see as promoting theft and murder, similar to gangsta rap in America. These criticisms have been deemed racist by the mostly Black British grime industry. Despite its controversial nature, grime has had a major affect on British fashion and pop music, with many young working class youth emulating the clothing worn by grime stars like Dizzee Rascal and Wiley. There are many subgenres of grime, including Rhythm and Grime, a mix of R&B and grime, and grindie, a mix of indie rock and grime popularized by indie rock band Hadouken.

Rap has globalized into many cultures worldwide, as evident through the emergence of numerous regional scenes. It has emerged globally as a movement based upon the main tennets of hip hop culture. The music and the art continue to embrace, even celebrate, its transnational dimensions while staying true to the local cultures to which it is rooted. Hip-hop's inspiration differs depending on each culture. Still, the one thing virtually all Hip Hop artists worldwide have in common is that they acknowledge their debt to those African American people in New York who launched the global movement. While hip-hop is sometimes taken for granted by Americans, it is not so elsewhere, especially in the developing world, where it has come to represent the empowerment of the disenfranchised and a slice of the American dream. American Hip-Hop music has reached the cultural corridors of the globe and has been absorbed and reinvented around the world.

GLITCH HOP AND WONKY MUSIC

Glitch Hop and Wonky music evolved following the rise of Trip Hop, dubstep and IDM. Both styles of music frequently reflect the experimental nature of IDM and the heavy bass featured in dubstep songs. While trip hop was described as being a distinct British upper-middle class take on Hip-Hop, glitch-hop and wonky music have featured much more stylistic diversity. Both genres are melting pots of influence, echoes of 1980s pop music, Indian ragas, eclectic jazz and West Coast rap can be heard in glitch Hop productions. Los Angeles, London, Glasgow and a number of other cities have become hot spots for these scenes, and underground scenes have developed across the world in smaller communities. Both genres often pay homage to more well older and more well established electronic music artists such as Radiohead, Aphex Twin and Boards of Canada as well as independent hip hop producers like J Dilla and Madlib.

Glitch Hop is a fusion genre of hip hop and glitch music that originated in the early to mid 2000s in the United States and Europe. Musically, it is based on irregular, chaotic breakbeats, glitchy basslines and other typical sound effects used in glitch music, like skips. Glitch Hop artists include Prefuse Dabrye and Flying Lotus.

CRUNK AND SNAP MUSIC

Crunk originated from southern hip hop in the late 1990s. The style was pioneered and commercialized by artists from Memphis, Tennessee and Atlanta, Georgia.

Looped, stripped-down drum machine rhythms are usually used. The Roland TR-808 and 909 are among the most popular. The drum machines are usually accompanied by simple, repeated synthesizer melodies and heavy bass stabs. The tempo of the music is somewhat slower than hip-hop, around the speed of reggaeton.

The focal point of crunk is more often the beats and music than the lyrics therein. Crunk rappers, however, often shout and scream their lyrics, creating an aggressive, almost heavy, style of hip-hop. While other subgenres of hip-hop address sociopolitical or personal concerns, crunk is almost exclusively party music, favoring call and response hip-hop slogans in lieu of more substantive approaches.

VOLUME TWO

INTRODUCTION

Hip hop began in the Bronx in New York City during the late 1970s. The origins of the word are often disputed. Some argue whether it started in the South or West Bronx. While the term hip hop is often used to refer only to hip hop music (also called rap), hip hop is four elements are considered essential to understand hip hop musically. Afrika Bambaataa of the hip hop collective, Zulu Nation outlined the pillars of hip hop culture, coining the terms: *"rapping" (also called MC or Microphone Commander), a rhythmic vocal rhyming style (orality), (turntablism), which is making music with record players and DJ mixers (aural/sound and music creation), b-boying/b-girling/break dancing (movement/dance), and graffiti art.* Other elements of hip hop subculture beyond the main four are: hip hop culture and historical knowledge of the movement (intellectual/philosophical); beat boxing, street entrepreneurship; hip hop language and street knowledge among others.

INTRODUCTION

Even as the hip hop movement continues to expand globally, the four foundational elements provide coherence and a strong foundation for hip hop culture. Hip hop is simultaneously a new and old phenomenon; the importance of sampling tracks, beats, and basslines from old records to the art form means that much of the culture has revolved around updating classic recordings, attitudes, and experiences for modern audiences. Sampling older culture and reusing it in a new context or a new format is called "flipping" in rap culture.

Hip hop follows in the footsteps of earlier African-American-rooted musical genres such as blues, jazz, rag-time, funk, and disco. It is the language known to urban environments of America. According to KRS-One, "Hip hop is the only place where you see Martin Luther King Jr.'s 'I Have a Dream Speech' in real life." KRS also mention that hip hop is beyond something as race, gender, or nationality; it belongs to the world.

In 1990, while working with the rap group "Snap!", Ronald "Bee-Stinger" Savage, a former member of the Zulu Nation, is credited for coining the term "Six Elements of the Hip-Hop Movement" by being inspired by Public Enemy's recordings. The elements are:

• Consciousness Awareness

• Civil Rights Awareness

• Activism Awareness

INTRODUCTION

- Justice

- Political Awareness

In the 2000s, with the rise of new media platforms and Web 2.0, fans discovered streamed hip hop through Myspace, YouTube, WorldStar Hip-Hop, SoundCloud, and Spotify.

CHAPTER ONE
ELEMENTS OF HIP-HOP

In the beginning, the house of Hip Hop was built on five fundamental pillars – MCing, DJing, Breakdance, Graffiti, and Knowledge. *A house built on rock must stand.* The pillars ushered Hip Hop into the 21st century as a cultural phenomenon was formulated by DJ Afrika Bambaataa of the hip-hop collective, Zulu Nation. The knowledge of the five elements might not be widespread, but its structural significance should not be understated. With a myriad of styles to hip hop, the *"elements provide coherence"* to the genre. Let's break them down:

1) DJing (aural) – This was a new found manipulation of sounds that was used to create music. The innovative breaks and isolation of the percussive beat gave hip hop its initial rise. Kool DJ Herc, who was the first to create hip hop in the 1970s, started this new form of DJing. In the early days, the DJs were the stars and later rappers such as Kurtis

Blow and Grand Master Flash with their ingenious rhymes took the spotlight.

2) MCing (oral) – Manifested from the social conditions of the time. This form of *"poetic and verbal acrobatics"* was derived from ancient African culture and oral tradition. Also known as "rapping" this element removed the veil that isolated the wider culture from the social conditions of many under-served urban communities. The rapid fire wordplay, spoke the truth of stories that weren't being told and gave rise to a new urban narrative.

3) Breakdance (physical) – Groups such as Shaka Zulu Kings, Zulu Queens and the Rock Steady Crew gave rise to B-Boying/B-Girling. Breaking can be described as "poetry in motion". Its acrobatics style with influences of gymnastics, Capoeira, martial arts and other cultural influences speaks to the innovative wave ushered in by hip hop culture.

4) Graffiti (visual) – This is one of the most controversial of the elements. As most graffiti artist leave their artwork in public places and "tag" it by leaving their names. TAKI 183, made this form of artistic representation famous and in neighborhoods such as Wynwood, Little Haiti and Opalocka, we can see this art form's widespread integration with bursts of energy and vibrancy on buildings throughout the cities.

5) Knowledge (mental) – This element is the thread that weaves all the other elements together. "Knowledge of self" refers to the Afro-diasporic mix of spiritual and political consciousness designed to empower members of oppressed groups," according Travis Gosa in his book entitled The Fifth Element of Hip Hop: Knowledge. This quote merges with the vision that Bambaataa had of hip-hop as a force for social change. Bambaataa states that "America has systematized our minds to be into materialism", but instead of buying into this notion, we should think about how we can give back to our communities.

Hip Hop is more than art, but a social movement that values art as a form of disrupting the norm and creating dialogue that encourages societal change.

CHAPTER TWO
HIP-HOP THROUGH THE
YEARS

In the 1980s, the next wave of musicians from New York came to light. At the forefront was Run-DMC, a trio of middle-class African Americans from Queens who fused rap with hard rock, defined a new style of hip dress, and became staples on MTV as they brought rap to a mainstream audience. They were signed to Profile Records, one of several new labels that took advantage of the growing market of rap artists.

Def Jam Records had three of the dopest hip-hop artists on their label; LL Cool J, rap's first romance rapper; the Beastie Boys, the first white hip-hop trio who broadened rap's audience and popularized digital sampling and Public Enemy, who rapped on African American social awareness similar to Grandmaster Flash and the Furious Five's song, "The Message" which was released in 1982.

During the Golden Era (1989–1993) De La Soul—whose

debut album on Tommy Boy Records, '3 Feet High and Rising' pointed hip hop in a more conscientious direction while female rappers such as Queen Latifah, MC Lyte and Salt-n-Pepa offered lyrics pointing to feminism, black awareness and female urban narratives. Hip-hop artists including DJ Jazzy Jeff and the Fresh Prince from Philly and M.C. Hammer, from Oakland raised the roof in pop, dance, and commercialism.

The most impactful response to New York's hip-hop scene, came from Los Angeles, beginning in 1989 with N.W.A.'s dynamic album, 'Straight Outta Compton.' N.W.A. (Niggaz With Attitude) —Ice Cube, Eazy E, MC Ren, DJ Yella and Dr. Dre—led the way as West Coast rap grew in prominence. Their graphic, violent tales of real life of the inner cities, and those of LA rappers such as Ice-T, MC Eiht, MC Breeze and of East Coast counterparts such as Schoolly D and the Hilltop Crew gave rise to the genre known as gangsta rap. In the early 1990s, Death Row Records built an empire around Dr. Dre, Snoop Dogg, and the rapper-actor Tupac Shakur, causing a rivalry with New York City's Bad Boy Records led by Sean "Puffy" Combs. This developed into a media-fueled hostility between East Coast and West Coast, which culminated in the still-unsolved murders of Shakur and Notorious B.I.G.

By the mid 1990s, hip-hop was artistically dominated by the Wu-Tang Clan, from New York City's Staten Island, Mobb Deep, Nas, Hit Squad, Diddy, Gangstarr, Biggy Smalls headed by Diddy- rapper, producer, and president of

Bad Boy Records, and the Fugees, who mixed pop music hooks with politics which later launched the careers of rappers, Wyclef Jean and Lauryn Hill.

Although long believed to be popular with urban African American males, hip-hop became the best-selling genre of popular music in the United States in the late 1990s. Its impact was global, with formidable audiences and artist pools in cities such as Paris, Tokyo, Sydney, Cape Town, London, and Bristol, England (where the spin-off trip-hop started). Hip Hop was responsible for generating huge sales in fashion, liquor, electronics, and automobiles that were popularized by its artists on MTV and The Box and in hip-hop-based publications such as The Source and Vibe. A canny blend of entrepreneurship and aesthetics, hip-hop was the wellspring of several staple techniques of modern pop music, including digital drumming and sampling (which introduced rap listeners to the music of a previous generation of performers, including Chic, Parliament-Funkadelic, and James Brown, while creating copyright controversies).

As the century turned, the music industry entered into a crisis, brought on by the advent of digitizing. Hip-hop suffered at least as severely as or worse than other genres, with sales tumbling. Simultaneously, though, it solidified its standing as the dominant influence on global youth culture. Even the popular "boy bands," such as the Backstreet Boys and *NSYNC, drew heavily on hip-hop sounds and styles, and rhythm and blues and gospel had adapted so fully to the newer approach that stars such as Mary J. Blige, R. Kelly, and Kirk Franklin straddled both worlds.

In the early 2000s, hip-hop's creative centre moved to the South. Following the success of the experimental OutKast and the stable of New Orleans-based artists that emerged from two record companies—Cash Money and No Limit Records (which was both founded and anchored by Master P)—the chant-based party anthems of such rappers as Juvenile, 8Ball & MJG, and Three 6 Mafia brought the sounds of the "Dirty South" to the forefront of rap music.

Back in New York, 50 Cent achieved multi-platinum status with 2003's album, 'Get Rich or Die Tryin' and Eminem, became perhaps the world's biggest rap star when 8 Mile (2002) enjoyed huge popular and critical success while his song, "Lose Yourself" won the Academy Award for best song. Both were proteges of Dr. Dre, former member of NWA. However, he started working behind the scenes on a brand new venture and didn't release an album after 1999.

Dr. Dre's legacy, though, was visible in the extent to which hip-hop had become a producers' medium. In the 21st century, the music—born from the sonic creations of the deejay—saw its greatest innovations in the work of such studio wizards as Timbaland, Swizz Beatz, and the Neptunes. The focus on producers as both a creative and a commercial force was concurrent with a widespread sense that the verbal dexterity and poetry of hip-hop was waning.

Hip-Hop had become associated with pop music, with the

intricacy and subversive nature of earlier MCs largely being pushed to the "alternative underground" scene spearheaded by rappers such as Mos Def and Doom. The dissatisfaction with the state of mainstream hip-hop was so common that in 2006, Nas released 'Hip Hop Is Dead'.

Still, major stars continued to emerge. Many of the biggest figures continued to rise from the South, including Atlanta's T.I. and Lil Wayne from New Orleans. Hip-hop celebritism now often came hand-in-hand with multimedia success, such as a burgeoning film career for rapper, Ludacris. The genre continued to be assimilated deeper into nonmusical culture, with some genre's early stars—LL Cool J, Ice Cube, Queen Latifah, Ice-T—established as familiar faces in movies and television. Snoop Dogg headlined rock festivals alongside Bruce Springsteen.

Perhaps no one represented the cultural triumph of hip-hop better than Jay-Z. As his career progressed, he went from performing artist to label president, head of a clothing line, club owner, and market consultant—along the way breaking Elvis Presley's Billboard magazine record for the most number-one albums by a solo artist. Barack Obama made references to Jay-Z during his 2008 presidential campaign. On Jay-Z's 2009 album "The Blueprint 3" he claimed to be a *"small part of the reason"* for Obama's victory.

Kanye West, one of Jay-Z's early producers, emerged as one of the most fascinating and polarizing characters in hip-hop following the success of his 2004 debut album 'The College Dropout.' Musically experimental and fashion-forward, West represented many of hip-hop's greatest possibilities with his penetrating, deeply personal lyrics. However, his political stances in recent times has caused outcry around the industry.

The music's global impact continued to expand. No single artist may have better personified hip-hop in the 21st century than M.I.A. M.I.A. wrote politically radical lyrics that are set to musical tracks that drew from diverse sources around the world. Not only was her album 'Kala' named the best album of 2007 by Rolling Stone, but M.I.A. was also listed as one of Time magazine's "100 Most Influential People"—illustrating the reach and power of a music born decades earlier on litter-strewn playgrounds.

CHAPTER THREE
DEFINITION OF RAPPING

Rapping (or rhyming, spitting, emceeing, MCing) is a musical form of vocal delivery that incorporates "rhyme, rhythmic speech, and street vernacular", which is performed or chanted in a variety of ways, usually over a backing beat or musical accompaniment. The components of rap include "content" (what is being said), "flow" (rhythm, rhyme), and "delivery" (cadence, tone). Rap differs from spoken-word poetry in that rap is usually performed in time to an instrumental track. Rap is often associated with, and is a primary ingredient of hip-hop music, but the origins of the phenomenon predate hip-hop culture. The earliest precursor to the modern rap is the West African griot tradition, in which "oral historians", or "praise-singers", would disseminate oral traditions and genealogies, or use their formidable rhetorical techniques for gossip or to "praise or critique individuals." Griot traditions connect to rap along a lineage of Black verbal reverence that goes back to ancient Egyptian practices, through James Brown interacting with the crowd and the band between songs, to Muhammad Ali's quick-witted verbal taunts and the palpitating poems of the Last Poets. Therefore, rap lyrics and music are part of the "Black rhetorical continuum", and aim to reuse elements of past traditions while expanding upon them through "creative use of language and rhetorical styles and strategies. The person credited with originating the style of "delivering rhymes over extensive music", that would become known as rap, was Anthony "DJ Hollywood" Holloway from Harlem, New York.

Rap is usually delivered over a beat, typically provided by a DJ, turntablist, beatboxer, or performed a cappella without accompaniment. Stylistically, rap occupies a gray area between speech, prose, poetry, and singing. The word, which predates the musical form, originally meant "to lightly strike", and is now used to describe quick speech or repartee. The word had been used in British English since the 16th century. It was part of the African American dialect of English in the 1960s meaning "to converse", and very soon after that in its present usage as a term denoting the musical style. Today, the term rap is so closely associated with hip-hop music that many writers use the terms interchangeably.

Rapping can be traced back to its African roots. Centuries

before hip-hop music existed, the griots of West Africa were delivering stories rhythmically, over drums and sparse instrumentation. Such connections have been acknowledged by many modern artists, modern day "griots", spoken word artists, mainstream news sources, and academics.

Blues music, rooted in the work songs and spirituals of slavery and influenced greatly by West African musical traditions, was first played by blacks and later by some whites, in the Mississippi Delta region of the United States around the time of the Emancipation Proclamation. Grammy-winning blues musician/historian Elijah Wald and others have argued that the blues were being rapped as early as the 1920s. Wald went so far as to call hip hop "the living blues." A notable recorded example of rapping in blues music was the 1950 song "Gotta Let You Go" by Joe Hill Louis.

Jazz, which developed from the blues and other African-American and European musical traditions and originated around the beginning of the 20th century, has also influenced hip hop and has been cited as a precursor of hip hop. Not just jazz music and lyrics but also jazz poetry. According to John Sobol, the jazz musician and poet who wrote Digitopia Blues, rap "bears a striking resemblance to the evolution of jazz both stylistically and formally". Boxer Muhammad Ali anticipated elements of rap, often using rhyme schemes and spoken word poetry, both for when he was trash talking in boxing and as political poetry for his activism outside of boxing, paving the way for The Last Poets in 1968, Gil Scott-Heron in 1970, and the emergence of rap music in the 1970s.

Precursors also exist in non-African/African-American traditions, especially in vaudeville and musical theater. One such tradition is the patter song exemplified by Gilbert and Sullivan but that has origins in earlier Italian opera. "Rock Island" from Meridith Wilson's The Music Man is wholly spoken by an ensemble of travelling salesmen, as are most of the numbers for British actor Rex Harrison in the 1964 Lerner and Loewe musical My Fair Lady. Glenn Miller's "The Lady's in Love with You" and "The Little Man Who Wasn't There" (both 1939), each contain distinctly rap-like sequences set to a driving beat as does the 1937 song "Doin' the Jive". In musical theater, the term "vamp" is identical to its meaning in jazz, gospel, and funk, and it fulfills the same function. Semi-spoken music has long been especially popular in British entertainment, and such examples as David Croft's theme to the 1970s' sitcom Are You Being Served? have elements indistinguishable from modern rap.

In classical music, semi-spoken music was popular stylized by composer Arnold Schoenberg as Sprechstimme, and famously used in Ernst Toch's 1924 Geographical Fugue for spoken chorus and the final scene in Darius Milhaud's 1915 ballet 'Les Choéphores'. In the French chanson field, irrigated by a strong poetry tradition, such singer-song-writers as Léo Ferré or Serge Gainsbourg made their own use of spoken word over rock or symphonic music from the very beginning of the 1970s. Although these probably did not have a direct influence on rap's development in the African-American cultural sphere, they paved the way for acceptance of spoken word music in the media market.

CHAPTER FOUR
HIP HOP'S TRENDSETTING GROUPS

The best rap groups come in various shades and sizes. Wu-Tang Clan set the bar high for the largest crews. De La Soul proved that three is the magic number. And groups like Beastie Boys and Cypress Hill showed that hip-hop has the power to bridge cultural gaps.

We've come to love crews like N.W.A. and Public Enemy because they changed the landscape of hip-hop with their activism and realism. We cherish OutKast and The Roots because they somehow pinched our hard-wiring and resonated with our humanity. Here are a few that come to mind.

CunninLynguists

CunninLynguists may be the best hip-hop group you've never heard of. Their style consists of southern-fried beats and gripping narratives that linger after the song ends. As forward-thinking as they are, they never managed to enjoy the mainstream exposure they deserve. Still, their pedigree is undeniable.

Members: Kno, Deacon The Villain, Natti

Little Brother

Influenced by Tribe Called Quest and De La, Little Brother took hip-hop by storm with their brand of brainy hip-hop. When BET deemed their "Lovin' It" video "too intelligent" for their audience, it further established LB as underground darlings. They went on to drop three great albums in three years, including 2007's GetBack.

Members: Phonte, Big Pooh, 9th Wonder

Slum Village

Though Slum Village had more lineup changes than Destiny's Child, quality remained a constant for the most part. The Detroit crew enjoyed a boost from the addition of lyricist Elzhi and a non-stop supply of thumping beats from Jay Dee.

Members: Baatin, Jay Dee, T3, Elzhi

. . .

Grandmaster Flash and the Furious Five

Flash and the Furious 5 are creative inventors in every sense, having influenced generations of MCs, b-boys, DJs, and style icons. "The Message" and "White Lines (Don't Do It)" helped launch what we now know as conscious rap. To crown it all, they made history as the first hip-hop act to be inducted into the Rock & Roll Hall of Fame. The only chink in their armor was their fashion steez -- glam cowboy hats, studded belts, Kangols and dukey rope chains.

Members: Grandmaster Flash, Melle Mel, Kid Creole, Cowboy, Scorpio (aka Mr. Ness) and Raheim

Naughty By Nature

Here's one oft-overlooked aspect of Naughty By Nature -- Treach could rap circles around his peers. He laced each song with a crisp new flow and made it seem effortless. The group's string of catchy hits would eventually propel them to mainstream success. In 1996, Naughty By Nature won the first ever Best Rap Album Grammy for Poverty's Paradise.

Members: Treach, DJ Kay Gee, and Vin Rock

Brand Nubian

Afrocentricity, spirituality, sexuality, self-empowerment,

you name it and Brand Nubian already rapped about it. No topic was off limits with these brothers, who occasionally dropped Five-percent knowledge.

Members: Lord Jamar, Sadat X, and Grand Puba

Three 6 Mafia

Before the hits, before the historic Oscar and TV shows, Triple 6 Mafia (DJ Paul, Juicy J) helped place Memphis on the map with their unique brand of donnybrook hip-hop. They've had no trouble selling records and making a mark in the land of Elvis.

Members: DJ Paul, Juicy J, and Lord Infamous

Cypress Hill

With the legendary DJ Muggs manning the board and B-Real offering street wisdom on the mic, Cypress Hill set the industry ablaze with three consecutive platinum albums. Granted, they were never able to match the intensity of their self-titled debut, arguably a street classic, but their impact is undeniable. The West Coast trio was inducted into the VH1 Hip-Hop Honors in 2008. (Brownie Points: Cypress Hill appeared in the "Homerpalooza" episode of The Simpsons)

Members: B-Real, DJ Muggs, Sen Dog, and Eric Bobo

The LOX

Mobb Deep and Capone-N-Noreaga were at the peak of their popularity in the late '90s, so The LOX could've easily been lost in the shuffle. Instead, the trio quickly pulled away from their New York peers with their edgy beats and intelligent rhymes. Jada's raspy voice added flavor to his rewind-worthy punchlines; Styles brought the straitjacket flow; while Sheek completed the cipher with a gritty delivery.

Members: Styles P, Jadakiss, and Sheek Louch

Goodie Mob

When Goodie Mob coined the term "dirty south," southern hip-hop was still taking a backseat to New York and L.A. However, Goodie Mob and OutKast carried the weight and helped place southern rap back on the map. "What Y'all fools know about the Dirty South?"

Members: Cee-Lo, Big Gipp, Khujo, and T-Mo

Hieroglyphics

When Del rhymed, "Life ain't all about busting caps or f--cking b--ches" on "At the Helm," he pretty much professed the group's mantra. Hiero was the first West Coast group to make a lasting impression without thuggin' on wax.

Members: Del tha Funkee Homosapien, Casual, Pep Love, A+, Opio, Tajai, Phesto, and Domino

Black Moon

We can't imagine many hip-hop heads without Black Moon's 1993 gemstone Enta Dah Stage in their collection. With Da Beatminerz and DJ Evil Dee supplying hardbody beats and Buckshot dropping dimes in his trademark raspy voice, Black Moon kept East Coast hip-hop on lock for years.

Members: Buckshot, DJ Evil Dee, 5ft Accelerator

Salt N Pepa

Salt 'N Pepa's contribution to hip-hop extends beyond their status as rap's most significant female group. They took the entire rap game by storm and grabbed the attention of both men and women with their titillating ditties.

Members: Salt, Pepa, Spinderella

Bone Thugs N Harmony

Show of hands if you ever caught yourself mimicking Bone

Thugs' melodic flow as a teenager. Yeah, me too. When these Midwest boys were Creepin on ah Come Up in the '90s, the game was rife with talented artists of all kinds from all regions. So, they created a sound that was both original and inimitable. Bone Thugs' blend of octane-fueled lyrics with harmonized vocals made them a household name.

Members: Krayzie Bone, Layzie Bone, Bizzy Bone, Wish Bone, Flesh-n-Bone

2 Live Crew

It's unfortunate that the hoopla over 2 Live Crew's sexually charged (sometimes misogynistic) songs eclipsed the group's musical accomplishment. The obscenity case over their 1989 LP, As Nasty as They Wanna Be, took them all the way to the Supreme Court. They weren't lyrical wizards, but their thunderous booty bops helped popularize the Miami bass sound. If this show is any indication, they're still as nasty as they wanna be.

Members: Luke, Fresh Kid Ice, Mr. Mixx, Amazing V., Brother Marquis, Verb

Geto Boys

Along with UGK and SUC, Geto Boys will always be revered as southern rap pioneers. Scarface delivered compelling stories about street life in Texas, while Willie D's impeccable mic presence and Bushwick Bill's maniacal rhymes kept things interesting. By all standards, the Geto boys paved the way for future southern hip-hop acts.

Members: Scarface, Bushwick Bill, Willie D

Fugees

The Fugees were a super talented bunch -- in fact, too talented for their own good. Though they would later have one of the most heartbreaking breakups after just two albums, they left an indelible impression on the music world. Their 1996 masterpiece, The Score, garnered so much buzz that it eventually eclipsed their first, though less remarkable CD, Blunted on Reality.

Members: Wyclef Jean, Lauryn Hill, Pras

Beastie Boys

Who knew that three white kids would eventually become one of hip-hop's most influential acts ever? The Beastie Boys were amongst the legion of trailblazers who left an indelible impression on a generation of rappers to follow. The Beastie Boys came out with a bang — dropping 1987's massive-selling Licensed to Ill. The group also reinvented its sound with the sample-heavy Paul's Boutique.

Members: Ad-Rock, Mike D, MCA

The Roots

Hip-hop's first legitimate band defies genres as well as comparisons. The Roots often rely heavily on live instrumentals and little on samples to create original, timeless hip-hop music. Besides, if you're in the market for the ultimate live show experience, your money's always safe with these Philly boys.

Members: Questlove, Black Thought, Kamal Gray, Captain Kirk, Frankie Knuckles, Tuba Gooding Jr.

De la Soul

While others were busy name-checking their gun collection, De La Soul positioned itself as the antithesis of everything gangsta rap represented. They were playful, intelligent, funny. Lyrically, they displayed maturity and vulnerability. Musically, they designed the manifesto that would alter the landscape of hip-hop forever.

Members: Posdnuos, Trugoy, Maseo

Public Enemy

While others were busy name-checking their gun collection, De La Soul positioned itself as the antithesis of everything gangsta rap represented. They were playful, intelligent, funny. Lyrically, they displayed maturity and vulnerability. Musically, they designed the manifesto that would alter the landscape of hip-hop forever.

Members: Posdnuos, Trugoy, Maseo

A Tribe Called Quest

Tribe was the most successful of their Native Tongues brethren, thanks, in part, to their consistency. By the time Tribe's third disc arrived, that brand of melodic, Crisco-slick classics that gave yield to "Electric Relaxation" and "Award Tour" had become synonymous with ATCQ.

Members: Ali Shaheed Muhammad, Q-Tip, Phife Dawg

Run DMC

Run-DMC's place as the most influential rap group and undeniably one of the greatest hip-hop acts of all-time is unquestionable. The trio shattered barriers for future generations with a bold and wildly innovative style of hip-hop that captivated fans from Queens to Macedonia. Run-DMC exemplified the perfect combination of honesty, attitude, and creativity.

Members: Run, DMC, Jam Master Jay

NWA

Any rapper who's made a buck by voicing social concerns without fear of castigation owes a royalty check to the world's most dangerous group. N.W.A. literally had to fight for their right to express themselves. Not even threats from the FBI could keep them from publicly indicting the powers that be or calling out racist cops. These Compton boys were vicious, unapologetic, and vividly outspoken. All good things, they say, must come to an end. Though N.W.A. finally broke up after 1991's Efil4zaggin, their legacy lived on. Dre, Cube, and Eazy would go on to launch successful solo careers respectively.

Members: Eazy-E, Dr. Dre, Ice Cube, MC Ren, DJ Yella, Arabian Prince

Wu-Tang Clan

The most powerful weapon in any group's arsenal is neither beats nor rhymes--not even one of those big head nodders that RZA used to make every 2 years. No weapon in hip-hop history can rival the chaotic cohesion of the Wu-Tang Clan. The Clan had so many characters, each with his own eccentricities. They were fearless in their approach. There's a good reason no group has been able to successfully recreate their sound. The crew spawned gazillions of loosely associated acts. Their classic albums spawned classic albums.

Members: RZA, GZA, Method Man, Raekwon, Ghostface Killah, Inspectah Deck, U-God, Masta Killa, ODB

Others worth considering:

- Jurassic 5
- Pharcyde
- Onyx
- The Beatnuts
- Freestyle Fellowship
- The Juice Crew

CHAPTER FIVE
80'S HIP HOP ARTISTS

2 Live Crew

3rd Bass

Audio Two

Antoinette

Beastie Boys

Big Daddy Kane

Biz Markie

Chubb Rock

Cold Crush Brothers

Cool C

De La Soul

DJ Jazzy Jeff & The Fresh Prince

DJ Kool Here

DJ Red Alert

Doug E. Fresh

Dana Dane

EPMD

Eric B & Rakim

The Fat Boys

Fearless Four

Funky 4 + 1

Gangstarr

Grandmaster Melly Mel

Heavy D

Ice-T

The Juice Crew

The Jungle Brothers

Just Ice

J.V.C. Force

Kid N Play

VOLUME TWO

Kid Frost

Kool G Rap

Kool Moe Dee

KRS-One

Kwame

Lady B

LL Cool J

Mantronix

Mark the 45 King

Marley Marl

MC Breeze

MC Hammer

MC Lyte

Monie Love

Newcleus

Nice n Smooth

N.W.A.

Public Enemy

Queen Latifah

ERIC REESE

Rakim

Rob Base

Roxanne Shante

The Real Roxanne

Run DMC

Schooly D

Salt-N-Pepa

Skinny Boys

Slick Rick

Special Ed

Steady B

Stetsasonic

Sugarhill Gang

Technotronic

The Sequence

Treacherous Three

Too Short

Tone Loc

Tuff Crew

UTFO

Ultramagnetic MCS

Whodini

World Class Wreckin' Cru

CHAPTER SIX
TOP HIP-HOP SONGS OF THE 1980S

The 1980s; a decade in which Hip Hop grew from a local phenomenon into a major worldwide musical and cultural force. Pioneered in New York City in the early 1970s, it was not until 1979 that the first Hip-Hop song was recorded and released – "Rapper's Delight" by the Sugarhill Gang. In the early 80's, Hip Hop artists released mainly singles and only from the mid-80s on – when the record labels got behind it – the world started to see regular album releases. From then on, Hip Hop quickly started spreading throughout the world. Here is a list of the top tracks in its genre during the 1980s:

1. Grandmaster Flash & The Furious Five - The Message (1982)

Perhaps the most important song in Hip Hop history. "The Message" was the first song with unabashed commentaries on life and society, and it had a huge influence on many conscious Hip Hop artists who came later.

2. Public Enemy - Rebel Without A Pause (1987)

"Rebel Without a Pause" was the first song created for and the first single released from Public Enemy's masterpiece It Takes a Nation of Millions to Hold Us Back. The song was released in 1987, way before the album came out in the summer of 1988, and it was sort of a bridge between the still somewhat unpolished sounds of Yo! Bum Rush The Show to the Bomb Squad produced perfection on It Takes A Nation. Instant classic.

3. Run DMC - Sucker MCs (1983)

First released in 1983, this was the B-side to Run DMC's first single "It's Like That". "Sucker MCs" was a perfect early indicator of the direction Hip Hop was going in. Harder, sparser beats and a new, more aggressive style of rapping. Run DMC is THE group that is responsible for bringing Hip Hop from the Old School to the Golden Age.

4. Eric B & Rakim - Microphone Fiend (1988)

This beat. These lyrics. PERFECTION. Strangely the single release of this track wasn't a huge success in 1988, but since then this track has rightfully come to be recognized not only as the quintessential Eric B & Rakim song but as one of Hip Hop's biggest songs ever as well.

5. Doug E Fresh & The Get Fresh Crew - The Show / La Di Da Di (1985)

These (double A-side) songs from Doug E Fresh & The Get Fresh Crew, featuring Slick Rick, are among the most classic tracks in Hip Hop, ever.

6. LL Cool J - Rock The Bells (1985)

From LL's groundbreaking debut album Radio, Rock The Bells will always be one of LL Cool J's signature tracks and a landmark track in Hip Hop history. Also, check out the original Rock The Bells version which did not appear on the Radio album. This version has LL spittin' rhymes over 7 minutes of hard-hitting, bells-infused Rick Rubin beats.

7. Public Enemy - Fight The Power (1989)

Arguably Public Enemy's best-known track, the musical theme for Spike Lee's classic movie Do The Right Thing is universally regarded as one of the best songs of all time. We agree.

8. Eric B & Rakim - I Ain't No Joke (1987)

This is what an opening track should sound like. Rakim immediately sets the tone for the rest of the album (and his career) with this brilliant song. After dropping their first two classic tracks – "Eric B Is President" and "My Melody" – in 1986, Eric B & Rakim really raised the bar in 1987 with Paid In Full – one of the top albums in all of Hip Hop's history.

9. Big Daddy Kane - Set It Off (1988)

The ultimate example of Big Daddy Kane's rapping prowess and lyrical skill. Pure, unadulterated Hip Hop – it doesn't get any better than this. One of the stand-out tracks of the all around masterful debut album Long Live The Kane.

10. Boogie Down Productions - My Philosophy (1988)

This track was so far ahead of its time, Hip Hop still hasn't caught up yet. Filled with Hip Hop Quotables, this song addresses the commercialization of Hip Hop and the rise of wack and fake rappers. Almost 30 years old and more relevant today than ever. Prophetic and brilliant, My Philosophy will always be considered one of Hip Hop's biggest songs EVER.

11. Run DMC - Peter Piper (1986)

The opening track to Run DMC's magnum opus Raising Hell and a tribute to the skills of the multi-talented Jam Master Jay. On this DJ-favorite, Run and DMC trade lyrics based on nursery rhymes and fairy tales while at the same time paying homage to JMJ's skills on the turntables. Perfect tag-team rhyming, perfect instrumental – perfect song.

12. Public Enemy - Black Steel In The Hour Of Chaos (1988)

This has to be one of the most impactful songs Public Enemy ever did, and that is saying something. A powerful story of a jailbreak, directed at the US government and its prison system. Hard-hitting lyrics, perfect instrumental – this is Public Enemy at its best.

13. Boogie Down Productions - South Bronx (1986)

In response to MC Shan's "The Bridge", Boogie Down Productions came out HARD with "South Bronx". It left no room for doubt about where Hip Hop originated nor who reigned supreme. An all-time classic Hip Hop anthem. The song was produced by DJ Scott La Rock, KRS-One and Ultramagnetic MCs' Ced Gee, and the first single of Boogie Down Productions' classic debut album Criminal Minded that would be released in 1987.

14. Audio Two - Top Billin' (1987)

Talk about a classic Hip Hop song. The brilliant reworking of the "Impeach The President" beat is simply unbeatable. Even if they never made any other real noteworthy music, Audio Two will forever be remembered because of this monumental track – released in 1987 as lead single for their otherwise disappointing 1988 album What More Can I Say?

15. N.W.A - Straight Outta Compton (1988)

N.W.A's Straight Outta Compton album was a game-changer; for better or for worse. One of the first real Gangsta Rap albums, going multi-platinum without any radio play. It influenced and changed the direction of Hip Hop, producing countless clones for decades to come. The difference between all the clones and this album is the originality and authenticity of Straight Outta Compton; combined with the revolutionary & flawless production of Dr Dre and the raw energy & at the time shocking lyrical imagery of Ice Cube, MC Ren & Eazy E. The album is a super classic and this title track the perfect opening salvo.

16. Slick Rick - Children's Story (1988)

After he made his imprint on the scene in 1985 on Doug e Fresh's classic songs "The Show" and "La Di Da Di", Slick Rick released his nearly flawless debut album The Great Adventures Of Slick Rick in 1988. Slick Rick's superior story telling abilities, combined with his humor and typical rap style shine on the whole album, this is the best song.

17. Kurtis Blow - The Breaks (1980)

Kurtis Blow was the first rapper to sign a contract with a major record label . "The Breaks" was the first Hip Hop single that went 'gold'. A hugely important and influential track.

18. Just Ice - Going Way Back (1987)

This track by Just Ice (with the help of a young KRS-One) deals with the origins of Hip Hop in the Bronx and the rest of New York. Just Ice names everyone that matters – a real Hip Hop history lesson.

19. Eric B & Rakim - Eric B Is President (1986)

Produced by Marley Marl, this is another landmark Hip

Hop song. The opening bars are among the most quoted in Hip Hop and the production is supremely creative and diverse. An enticing introduction to the album that would come out the following year and would turn out to be one of the biggest classics in Hip Hop history.

20. LL Cool J - I'm Bad (1987)

LL Cool J at his bragging and boasting best, "I'm Bad" will always be one of LL's most recognizable songs and one of his biggest hits.

21. Ice T - 6 N The Morning (1986)

Inspired by arguably the first 'gangsta rap' song – 1985's "PSK What Does It Mean" by Philly rapper Schoolly D, Ice T's "6 N The Morning" is one of the most influential songs in Hip Hop as it more or less gave precedence to gangsta rap. As the media portrayed most gangsta rappers as tough-guy posturing, gun-toting idiots, somehow, Ice T found a balance that attracted consumers. He always combined authenticity with humor, displaying a calm confidence without the need to prove anything.

22. Funky 4 Plus 1 - That's The Joint (1980)

This is a classic single from the first Hip Hop group ever to get a record deal. Also, this is the first group with a female rapper to record a single. No doubt you've heard samples from this classic track in later Hip Hop favorites many times.

23. Schoolly D - PSK, What Does It Mean? (1985)

One of the first songs that was labeled 'gangsta rap' and THE track that inspired Ice T to write 6 N The Morning. Hugely influential, this is an all-time classic by Philly legend Schoolly D.

24. Ice T - Colors (1988)

The powerful title track of the classic 1988 movie "Colors", will forever be one of Ice T's best tracks.

25. Boogie Down Productions - Criminal Minded (1987)

Just one of the classic tracks of Criminal Minded. Clever lyrics, a banging instrumental – this song, along with the rest of the album, was crucial in the maturing of Hip Hop and was one of the albums (together with Run DMC's 'Raising Hell', Eric B & Rakim's 'Paid in Full', Public Enemy's 'Yo! Bum Rush The Show' and LL Cool J's first two albums) that started Hip Hop's Golden Age.

26. Beastie Boys - Paul Revere (1986)

The bass-line and reverse beat on this song are just crazy. Co-written by Run DMC and Rick Rubin, the song is a fictional and humorous account of how the Beastie Boys met. Pure genius.

27. Public Enemy - Don't Believe The Hype (1988)

P.E.'s classic critique of false media and rumors is yet another winner from their monumental sophomore album.

Classic beat, classic rhymes, classic hook. Don't Believe The Hype

28. Ultramagnetic MCs - Ego Trippin' (1986)

The original version of one of the centerpieces of Ultramagnetic MCs' underrated 1988 masterpiece Critical Beatdown was recorded as early as 1986. A super innovative and absolute classic track.

29. MC Lyte - Cha Cha Cha (1989)

"Cha Cha Cha" is the first single from MC Lyte's second album Eyes on This. No doubt one of MC Lyte's very best songs, this is 100% pure Hip Hop.

30. N,W.A - Fuck Tha Police (1988)

One of the most controversial songs in Hip Hop ever? The sad thing is that in the almost 30 years since this song was recorded nothing has changed with police relations in urban communities.

31. Stop The Violence Movement - Self Destruction (1989)

Remember the days Hip Hop was all about consciousness and improvement? The Stop the Violence Movement was started by KRS-One in response to violence in the Hip Hop and African American communities. With an East Coast all-star line-up, it was one of 1989's biggest songs, one that resonates with relevance to this day.

32. Eric B & Rakim - Paid In Full (1987)

The memorable bass line and Rakim's classic bars – surely one of the most potent verses ever – assure that this song is one of the most recognizable joints in the history of Hip Hop. Who doesn't have the words to this one memorized?

33. The Treacherous Three - Body Rock (1980)

The Treacherous Three is a crew of Hip Hop pioneers from who Kool Moe Dee is the best known. "Body Rock" is a typical song of the time: long and full of that Old School style of rapping . The first Hip Hop song to use rock influences.

34. De La Soul - Buddy (1989)

"Buddy" is the third single from De La Soul's classic debut album 3 Feet High and Rising. Great vibe and great lyrics – humorous and full of double entendres. The video version features the Jungle Brothers, Q-Tip & Monie Love. The original, also included on 3 Feet High & Rising, is dope as well.

35. Eric B & Rakim - Follow The Leader (1988)

Five minutes of lyrical perfection. Together with "Lyrics of Fury", perhaps one of the best examples of how advanced Rakim was with his lyricism. Listen to it and then listen to it again and let it sink in. Rakim will take the listener on a metaphorical trip into outer-space and then back into the listeners head. A lyrical masterpiece.

36. Public Enemy - Public Enemy No. 1 (1987)

Public Enemy's debut single. Remember, this was 1987. Musically, nothing like this was done before, ever. Highly innovative, this unique sound would become trademark Public Enemy. Throw Chuck D's booming voice and his back-and-forth with joker Flavor Flav in the mix and the signature sound of one of Hip Hop biggest acts ever is born.

37. EPMD - You Gots To Chill (1988)

You Gots To Chill is the quintessential EPMD song. It introduced the world to the laidback funk-laced Hip Hop of EPMD – and is just as timeless a classic as the album it came from, Strictly Business.

38. Beastie Boys - Shake Your Rump (1989)

Everything that makes Paul's Boutique so brilliant comes together on this track. The album performed commercially disappointing upon release (people were probably expecting more Fight For Your Right style frat-rap), but Paul's Boutique would eventually universally be recognized as the creative and innovative masterpiece that it is.

39. Stetsasonic - Talkin'All That Jazz (1988)

This under-appreciated song is a response to critics of (sampling in) Hip Hop. The stand-out track from Stetsasonic's solid second album In Full Gear.

40. Boogie Down Productions - The Bridge Is Over (1987)

Directed at the Juice Crew, and in response to MC Shan's Kill That Noise, this is the final jab on wax in the Bridge Wars. Brilliantly hard in its simplicity, it is instantly recognizable because of the menacing beat, sharp drum kicks and classic piano melody

41. EPMD - So Whatcha Sayin' (1989)

Picking the perfect opening track for an album is an art EPMD understood well. They got it right on their first album and did it again on their second one. So Whatcha Sayin' is perfect for setting the tone for the rest of Unfinished Business, which would turn to be just as awesome an album as EPMD's debut was.

42. MC Lyte - Paper Thin (1988)

An emcee who can spit with the best of them, male or female. MC Lyte's debut album still is a classic piece of work, that belongs in any Hip Hop fan's collection. "Paper Thin" is the now classic cut with which Lyte made her mark.

43. MC Shan - The Bridge (1986)

The song that started the legendary "Bridge Wars" and elicited a few vicious responses from KRS One's Boogie Down Productions, who responded to Shan's alleged claim that Hip Hop started out in Queens. Even though the intention of "The Bridge" may not even have been to make that claim, it still is responsible for one of the first beefs in Hip Hop and a few classic BDP songs. Of course, the

Marley Marl-produced "The Bridge" is a classic song in its own right.

44. N.W.A - Dopeman (Original) (1987)

From the same album as Eazy-E's original version of "Boyz N The Hood", this track was the no holds barred introduction of N.W.A to the world, with some classic Ice Cube lyrics and revolutionary production by a young Dr Dre.

45. Biz Markie - Vapors (1988)

The lead single from Biz Markie's full-length debut album Goin' Off. In full story-telling mode Biz shows us how people's behavior changes after you become successful. Classic.

46. Eric B & Rakim - Move The Crowd (1987)

Rakim took braggadocios rhyming to a new level by adding an intellectual veneer to it all – nobody could say "I'm the best" the way Rakim did, dismissing all competition casually and effortlessly and always without the use of profanity.

47. Biz Markie - Make The Music With Your Mouth, Biz (1986)

Another Marley Marl produced classic, this one from Biz Markie – who started out beat boxing for Roxanne Shante but soon crafted his own career – as a solo artist, as part of the Juice Crew and as close associate of longtime friend Big Daddy Kane (who soon had his own mark to make on the

Hip Hop game). This song was the lead track for a 1986 EP and would also be included on Biz Markie's 1988 full-length debut Goin' Off.

48. Eazy E - Boyz N The Hood (1988)

This revamped version for Eazy E's debut album 'Eazy Duz It' is even better than the 1987 original. Another classic Dr Dre production.

49. Big Daddy Kane - Smooth Operator (1989)

One of Big Daddy Kane's biggest hits and best-known songs. Showcasing his ladies-man persona to the fullest and lyrically destroying the competition at the same time, Smooth Operator is signature Big Daddy Kane. As smooth as it gets.

50. Eric B & Rakim - My Melody (1986)

Yet another Marley Marl produced classic with Rakim spitting elite bars over a hypnotic, slow and hard-ass beat. The rhyming and wordplay here are absolutely amazing and classic if only for the '7 emcees' bars, which are among the most notable in Hip Hop EVER.

51. The D.O.C. – It's Funky Enough (1989)

52. Eric B & Rakim – Lyrics Of Fury (1988)

53. Grandmaster Flash & The Furious Five – New York New York (1983)

54. Run DMC – Darryl & Joe (1985)

55. Big Daddy Kane – Ain't No Half Steppin' (1988)

56. Ice T – Squeeze The Trigger (1987)

57. Roxanne Shante – Bite This (1985)

58. LL Cool J – I Can't Live Without My Radio (1985)

59. Marley Marl – The Symphony (1988)

60. Afrika Bambaataa – Planet Rock (1982)

61. Ice T – You Played Yourself (1989)

62. Special Ed – I Got It Made (1989)

63. Fearless Four – Rockin It (1982)

64. Run DMC – Beats To The Rhyme (1988)

65. Public Enemy – Night Of The Living Baseheads (1988)

66. Grandmaster Melle Mel & The Furious Five – White Lines (1983)

67. Just Ice – Cold Gettin' Dumb (1986)

68. Gang Starr – Manifest (1989)

69. UTFO – Leader Of The Pack (1985)

70. J.V.C. Force – Strong Island (1987)

71. Queen Latifah ft Monie Love – Ladies First (1989)

72. Big Daddy Kane – Warm It Up Kane (1989)

73. Stetsasonic – Go Stetsa I (1986)

74. DJ Jazzy Jeff & The Fresh Prince – Brand New Funk (1988)

75. Grandmaster Melle Mel & The Furious Five – Step Off (1984)

76. Kool G Rap & DJ Polo – Road To The Riches (1989)

77. Biz Markie – Just A Friend (1989)

78. Slick Rick – Hey Young World (1988)

79. Mantronix – Bassline (1985)

80. Kool G Rap & DJ Polo – It's A Demo (1986)

81. Boogie Down Productions – You Must Learn (1989)

82. Run DMC – King Of Rock (1985)

83. De La Soul – Say No Go (1989)

84. Ultramagnetic MCs – Watch Me Now (1988)

85. Run DMC – My Adidas (1986)

86. Grandmaster Melle Mel & The Furious Five – Beat Street (1984

87. Tuff Crew – My Part Of Town (1988)

88. Big Daddy Kane – Raw (1987 / 1988)

89. Cold Crush Brothers – Fresh, Wild, Fly & Bold (1984)

90. N.W.A – Express Yourself (1988)

91. Run DMC – It's Like That (1983)

92. Kool Moe Dee – Go See The Doctor (1986)

93. The D.O.C. – The Formula (1989)

94. 3rd Bass – Brooklyn Queens (1989)

95. Beastie Boys – The New Style (1986)

96. Public Enemy – Bring The Noise (1987)

97. LL Cool J – Jack The Ripper (1988)

98. Treacherous Three – The New Rap Language (1980)

99. Rob Base & DJ EZ Rock – It Takes Two (1988)

100. Fat Boys – Stick Em (1984)

CHAPTER SEVEN
TOP HIP-HOP ALBUMS OF THE 1980S

1. Public Enemy - It Takes A Nation Of Millions To Hold Us Back (1988)

"Yes – the rhythm, the rebel / Without a pause – I'm lowering my level / The hard rhymer – where you never been I'm in…" (Rebel Without A Pause)

Public Enemy's 'It Takes A Nation Of Millions To Hold Us Back' is one of the best albums ever made, in any genre. The best and one of the most important Hip Hop albums ever. Enough said.

Top tracks: Rebel Without A Pause | Bring The Noise | Don't Believe The Hype | Black Steel In The Hour Of Chaos

2. Eric B & Rakim - Paid In Full (1987)

"This is how It should be done. This style is identical to none..." (I Know You Got Soul)

In a music genre still in its infancy, this Eric B & Rakim masterpiece was a game changer. Seductive, smooth yet hard beats laced with Rakim's innovative and intricate rhyme style, make for this groundbreaking and seminal work. This is one album that can be seen as a precursor to 1988, Hip Hop's break-out year. An album that established Hip Hop as a musical genre that was there to stay. Paid In Full will forever be recognized as one of Hip Hop's ultimate classics. Filled with unforgettable tracks and Hip Hop anthems this album is a must-have. If you don't own this album, your Hip Hop collection is incomplete.

Top tracks: I Ain't No Joke | My Melody | Eric B Is President | Move The Crowd

3. Ultramagnetic MCs - Critical Beatdown (1988)

"Well I'm the ultimate, the rhyme imperial / I'm better, but some don't believe me though / But I'm a pro in hot material / On your Walkman, box or any stereo" (Watch Me Now)

A classic album that has stood the test of time – Kool Keith's unique style & lyrics along with the excellent overall production ensure this is one for the ages. Highly original & innovative and very consistent – no weak tracks here. Critically acclaimed, but slept on and somehow under-appreciated – this is one of HHGA's all-time favorite albums and deserves its top spot in this list of Hip Hop's break-out decade.

Top tracks: Ego Trippin' | Ease Back | Watch Me Now | Funky

4. Boogie Down Productions - Criminal Minded (1987)

"We're not promoting violence, we're just having some fun – he's Scott La Rock, I'm KRS One" (Criminal Minded)

After making a name for themselves in the NYC Hip Hop underground, former social worker Scott La Rock and one of his clients, KRS One, formed Boogie Down Productions and came out in 1987 with Criminal Minded. The sparse production by the artists – and the at the time uncredited Ced Gee of the Ultramagnetic MCs – combined with KRS One's lyrical content and distinctive delivery make this album a definitive Hip Hop classic, that without a doubt is up there with the greatest Hip Hop albums of all time. Together with other groundbreaking 1987 debuts of Eric B & Rakim (Paid In Full) and Public Enemy (Yo! Bum Rush The Show), this album set the standard for Golden Age of Hip Hop.

Top Tracks: The Bridge Is Over | South Bronx | Criminal Minded | Poetry

5. De La Soul - 3 Feet High And Rising (1989)

"Mirror, mirror on the wall / Tell me, mirror, what is wrong? /

Can it be my De La clothes / Or is it just my De La song?" (Me, Myself & I)

Innovative and hugely influential – this cooperation between De La Soul and producer Prince Paul is truly a landmark album in Hip Hop. This album introduced the skit to Hip Hop albums; and although skits more often irritate than add value, on this album they work. The whole album is consistent and all the songs are awesome. Clever wordplay, deft rhymes, playful production, positivity and fun: 3 Feet High And Rising represented a new direction for Hip Hop, clearly a reaction to cliches already emerging in Hip Hop, even in its early years. De La Soul's debut is a must have for anyone who loves Hip Hop and an all-time classic.

Top tracks: The Magic Number | Say No Go | Eye Know | Ghetto Thang

6. Slick Rick - The Great Adventures Of… (1988)

"Gather 'round party go-ers as if you're still livin / And get on down to the old Slick rhythm" (The Ruler's Back)

It doesn't get much better than this. A flawless album from start to finish, filled with dope tracks. Slick Rick's superior story telling abilities, combined with his humor and typical rap style, make this album an unforgettable classic.

Top tracks: Mona Lisa | The Ruler's Back | Hey Young World | Children's Story

7. N.W.A. - Straight Outta Compton (1988)

"Straight outta Compton, crazy motherfucker named Ice Cube / From the gang called Niggaz With Attitudes..." (Straight Outta Compton)

This album was a game-changer. One of the first real 'gangsta rap' albums, and one of the most successful, going multi-platinum with no radio play. It influenced and changed the direction of Hip Hop, producing countless clones for decades to come. The difference between all the clones and this album is the originality and authenticity of Straight Outta Compton; combined with the revolutionary & flawless production of Dr Dre and the raw energy & at the time shocking lyrical imagery of Ice Cube, MC Ren & Eazy E. Super classic.

Top tracks: Straight Outta Compton | Fuck Tha Police | Gangsta Gangsta | Express Yourself

8. Run DMC - Raising Hell (1986)

"Kings from Queens, from Queens come Kings / We're raising hell like a class when the school bell rings..."

One of the first mega-sellers in Hip Hop and the album that would cement the status of Run DMC as most important Hip Hop act of the time. A brilliant album, with perfect interplay between Jam Master Jay – one of the first great all round DJ's in the game – and the back-and-forth rhyming of DMC and Run. This album, together with Beastie Boys' debut Licensed To Ill from the same year, opened Hip Hop to all kinds of audiences all over the world. Run DMC "took the beat from the street and put it on TV".

Top tracks: Peter Piper | Raising Hell | My Adidas | It's Tricky

9. LL Cool J - Radio (1985)

"LL Cool J is hard as hell / Battle anybody / I don't care who you tell..." (Rock The Bells)

LL Cool J's debut album is one of the most influential Hip Hop albums of all time. Together with Run DMC's debut album from the year before, Radio was the second album that would set the tone for how Hip Hop would sound. Rick Rubin's stripped-down, minimalistic production complements LL Cool J B-Boy attitude and revolutionary lyricism perfectly. This is one of the greatest and most important debuts in the history of Hip Hop and LL Cool J is one of the all-time greats.

Top tracks: Rock The Bells | I Can't Live Without My Radio | Dangerous | You'll Rock

10. Beastie Boys - Paul's Boutique (1989)

"Now I rock a house party at the drop of a hat / I beat a biter down with an aluminum bat / a lot of people they be Jonesin' just to hear me rock the mic / they'll be staring at the radio / staying up all night" (Shake Your Rump)

Was there ever an album, in any genre, that used sampling

more brilliantly and creatively than Paul's Boutique? This album truly is sampling heaven. Paul's Boutique differed completely from Beastie Boys' much easier accessible and commercially super successful debut album 'Licensed To Ill'; and not what a lot of fans of that album were expecting. Initially a commercial failure, Paul's Boutique aged like fine wine and with it the appreciation for it. Now considered a landmark album in Hip Hop, it's the ultimate example for what the Beastie Boys always stood for: creativity and innovation. They were never afraid to reinvent themselves and stretch (and cross) genre boundaries, while at the same time keeping it real. A timeless masterpiece, we will forever remember Paul's Boutique as a classic album, in music, not just in Hip Hop.

Top tracks: Shake Your Rump | Hey Ladies | Shadrach | B-Boy Bouillabaisse

11. Run DMC - Run DMC (1984)

"You five dollar boy and I'm a million dollar man / You'se a sucker emcee, and you're my fan" (Sucker MCs)

This album would be the one to change the direction of Hip Hop. Going for rock-infused, stripped-down, hard beats and a new kind of emceeing, it was game-changing in more ways than one. A great prelude to even greater things to come. The new standard.

Top tracks: Sucker MCs | Jam Master Jay | Hollis Crew | Rock Box

12. Big Daddy Kane - Long Live The Kane (1988)

"Let it roll, get bold, I just can't hold / Back, or fold cos I'm a man with soul / In control and effect, so what the heck / Rock the discotheque and this groove is what's next" (Set It Off)

With Big Daddy Kane's debut album, he established himself as one of Hip Hop's top lyricists. Marley Marl produced this album at the peak of his powers and is a definitive Hip Hop classic.

Top tracks: Raw | Set It Off | Ain't No Halfsteppin' | Long Live The Kane

13. The DOC - No One Can Do It Better (1989)

"Keepin' it dope as long as I can like imagine / Makin' each record that I do better than the last one" (The Formula)

On the heels of the explosive success of N.W.A's Straight Outta Compton, Dr Dre produced another flawless album but this time for a solo emcee by the name of The D.O.C. He was a lyrical and a rare-breed for the West Coast Rap scene. He co-wrote many of N.W.A's pieces especially for Eazy-E and is one of the co-founders of Death Row Records. The D.O.C. was born in Dallas, Texas but was raised in Los Angeles.

Top tracks: It's Funky Enough | The Formula | Mind Blowin' | The Grand Finale

14. Eric B & Rakim - Follow The Leader (1988)

"I was a fiend before I became a teen / I melted microphone instead of cones of ice cream / Music orientated so when Hip Hop was originated / Fitted like pieces of puzzles, complicated" (Microphone Fiend)

Faced with the impossible task to follow up the game-changing classic Paid In Full, Eric B & Rakim delivered, anyway. Rakim raised the bar of emceeing to a level few ever approached.

Top tracks: Microphone Fiend | Follow The Leader | Lyrics Of Fury | Musical Massacre

15. Boogie Down Productions - By All Means Necessary (1988)

"See I'm telling, and teaching pure facts / The way some act in rap is kind of wack / And it lacks creativity and intelligence / But they don't care cause their company's selling it" (My Philosophy)

Not even one year after Boogie Down Productions' classic debut album Criminal Minded, and shortly after the murder of Scott La Rock, KRS One drops another classic. KRS One quickly establishes himself as the conscious voice of Hip Hop, together with Public Enemy – a role both acts would maintain in the decades to follow.

Top tracks: My Philosophy | Ya Slippin' | I'm Still No. 1 | Stop The Violence

16. Public Enemy - Yo! Bum Rush The Show (1987)

"Well I'm all in / put it up on the board / another rapper shot down from the mouth that roared / 1-2-3 down for the count / the result of my lyrics, oh yes, no doubt" (Public Enemy No. 1)

The classic debut of one of Hip Hop's greatest and most important groups of all time. This album truly was a game-changer, production- and content-wise. Rough, hard-hitting beats and turntablism, complemented by Chuck D's booming voice and Flavor Flav's antics – Yo! Bum Rush The Show was revolutionary in many ways. Hugely influential and the stepping stone to Public Enemy's follow up and Hip Hop's ultimate classic album: It Takes A Nation Of Millions To Hold Us Back.

Top Tracks: You're Gonna get Yours | My Uzi Weighs A Ton |Timebomb | Public Enemy No. 1

17. EPMD - Strictly Business (1988)

"Relax your mind, let your conscience be free / And get down to the sounds of EPMD" (You Gots To Chill)

Consistent quality. Two words that describe the work of EPMD. EPMD's first album delivered the goods: funky beats and dope rhymes – it established EPMD as one of the true powerhouses in Hip Hop.

Top tracks: Strictly Business | You Gots To Chill | Get Off The Bandwagon | Let The Funk Flow

18. Beastie Boys - Licensed To Ill (1986)

A timeless classic. Licensed To Ill is pure energy and great fun. The Beastie Boys were the first white act in Hip Hop to make it big and maintain credibility and respect in the Hip Hop world throughout their career. This album is another one of the big, early successes of Def Jam – the dominating and most innovating record label at the time, extremely important for the exposure of Hip Hop to larger audiences worldwide.

Top tracks: Paul Revere | The New Style | Rhymin And Stealin | Hold It Now, Hit It

19. Kool G Rap & DJ Polo - Road To The Riches

"Bass, snare drum in your eardrum / Musical outcome, lyrical tantrum / Energy enters me, power absorbed / Phonograph arts and crafts mic warlord" (Rhymes I Express)

Kool G Rap is generally considered one of the greatest emcees ever, a pioneer of multi-syllabic & internal rhymes and complex rhyme schemes. One of the best spitters ever and next to Rakim. Later, Kool G Rap would start what was known as 'mafioso' rap, but here he was a straight up emcee with mostly braggadocio, battle-ready rhymes over Marley Marl's sparse beats. Kool G Rap is often named your favorite rapper's favorite rapper, and this album shows why.

Top tracks: Road To The Riches | Butcher Shop | Rhymes I Express | Poison

20. LL Cool J - Bigger And Deffer (1987)

"No rapper can rap quite like I can – I'll take a musclebound man and put his face in the sand" (I'm Bad)

Still early days in Hip Hop, but LL Cool J already comes out with his sophomore album. One of the first megasellers in Hip Hop (together with 1986 albums Raising Hell from Run DMC & Licensed To Ill from the Beastie Boys). LL Cool J at the top of his game.

Top tracks: I'm Bad | The Doo Wop | Go Cut Creator Go | The Breakthrough

21. Ice T - Power (1988)

"I'm livin' large as possible, posse unstoppable / Style topical, vividly optical" (Power)

Power, Ice T's second studio album, is an excellent follow up to his 1987 debut Rhyme Pays. Dope beats & lyrics which carried Ice T's personality – this is a classic album that definitely has stood the test of time. Top tracks: Power | High Rollers | Personal | Drama

22. EPMD - Unfinished Business (1989)

"My father always told me to wisen up son / Cause if you hung with nine broke friends, you're bound to be the 10th one" (It Wasn't Me, It Was The Fame)

No sophomore slump for EPMD. One year after their brilliant debut album Strictly Business they turned out another classic. A tight album from start to finish, Unfinished Business proved EPMD's consistency. Top tracks: So Whatcha

Sayin' | The Big Payback | Strictly Snappin' Necks | It Wasn't Me, It Was The Fame

23. Jungle Brothers - Straight Out The Jungle (1988)

"Educated man, from the motherland / You see, they call me a star but that's not what I am / I'm a jungle brother, a true, blue brother / And I've been to many places you'll never discover" (Straight Out The Jungle)

The debut album of the Jungle Brothers, and the first album of a group affiliated with The Native Tongues collective. An influential album – it marked the beginning of a series of albums by groups like De La Soul, A Tribe Called Quest and Black Sheep. Dope production, mellow rhymes – another 1988 classic. Top tracks: Straight Out The Jungle | On The Run | Because I Got it Like That | What's Going On

24. MC Lyte - Lyte As A Rock (1988)

"This thing called Hip Hop, Lyte is ruling it / I hate to laugh in your face, but you're funny / Your beat, your rhyming, your timing, all crummy" (10% Diss)

A female emcee who can spit with the best, male or female. MC Lyte's debut album still is a classic piece of work, that belongs in any Hip Hop fan's collection. Top tracks: Paper Thin | 10% Diss | I Cram To Understand U | Kickin' 4 Brooklyn

25. Ice T - Rhyme Pays (1987)

"6 in the morning, police at my door, fresh Adidas squeak across the bathroom floor" (6 N The Morning)

Even with a sometimes uneven production and an Ice T who hasn't quite reached the peaks of his lyrical skills yet – this album is an undeniable classic. Very influential (for good or for bad), it was one of the very first albums with 'gangsta rap' themes (although with limited profanity). In 1987, the gangsta theme had originality and authenticity, which makes Ice T a true O.G. & a bonafide Hip Hop icon. Top tracks: 6 N The Morning | Pain | Squeeze The Trigger | Rhyme Pays

26. Schoolly D - Saturday Night The Album (1987)

"It was Saturday night and I was feeling kinda funny, gold around my neck, pockets full of money" (Saturday Night)

Philadelphia rapper, Schoolly D was all about attitude. Though not the best rapper ever to spit rhymes, he dropped some pioneer albums in the mid-'80s and carried them with his grit and grime. This second album shows Schoolly D in top form – hardcore lyrics over minimalist, hard-hitting beats. The first two Schoolly D albums belong in any Hip Hop fans' music collection. Top Tracks: Saturday Night | B-Boy & Rhyme Riddle | Dis Groove Is Bad | Parkside 5-2

27. Boogie Down Productions - Ghetto Music: The Blueprint Of Hip Hop (1989)

"I believe that if you're teaching history / Filled with straight

up facts no mystery / Teach the student what needs to be taught / 'Cause Black and White kids both take shorts / When one doesn't know about the other ones' culture / Ignorance swoops down like a vulture..." (You Must Learn)

By 1989, BDP had already two very different, but equally classic albums out. This third effort only cemented BDP's and KRS One's prominence in Hip Hop. KRS One firmly establishes himself as Hip Hop's No.1 conscious voice; a role he fills to this day.

Top tracks: Why Is That? | Bo! Bo! Bo! | You Must Learn | Jack Of Spades

28. Geto Boys - Grip It! On That Other Level (1989)

"I'm back like a rebel 'making trouble' / I'm an Assassin, kickin ass on the double / No motherfucker alive's gonna stop me / So fuck you and your goddamn posse" (Do It Like A G.O.)

This is Geto Boys' second album, but the first one with the current line-up: Scarface, Willie D & Bushwick Bill (plus DJ Ready Red). This album is as groundbreaking as NWA's Straight Outta Compton – with it's violent and misogynistic topics. The beats are excellent and the emcees are dope. The album that put Houston Hip Hop on the map.

Top tracks: Mind Of A Lunatic | Do It Like A G.O. | Scarface | Size Ain't Shit

29. Eazy E - Eazy Duz It (1988)

"Woke up quick, at about noon / Jus' thought that I had to be in Compton soon" (Boys N The Hood)

Eazy E's debut album really is a veiled N.W.A. album. The lyrics are written by Ice Cube, The D.O.C. and MC Ren, who also makes a few appearances. The production is handled by Dr Dre & DJ Yella– this clearly is a group effort. A little less consistent than N.W.A.'s Straight Outta Compton – released in the same year – this album still is a bonafide (West Coast) Hip Hop classic.

Top tracks: Boys N The Hood | Eazy Duz It | Eazy-er Said Than Dunn | We Want Eazy

30. Stetsasonic - On Fire (1986)

"When we're coolin' on the block, we carry our big box / Playin L.L.'s 'Rock the Bells' or Run's 'Rock Box' / Wearin some high-top Cons or some Fila socks / And the newest Benetton sweat-shirt in stock…" (On Fire).

The first Hip-Hop band: Stetsasonic came out with a bang with this album in 1986. Fine work from a young Prince Paul on the boards and great synergy between Stet's emcees – this is an essential 80s Hip Hop album. Top tracks: On Fire | My Rhyme | 4 Ever My Beat | Just Say Stet

31. Ice T - The Iceberg (1989)

"Cos I'm the coldest motherfucker that you ever heard / Call me The Ice…or just The Iceberg" (The Iceberg)

Ice-T's grittiest album, but one with great variation lyrically and sonically. From the epic, ominous intro "Shut Up, Be Happy" (featuring Jello Biafra and brilliantly interpolating Black Sabbath's classic "Black Sabbath") to the all-out fun "My Word Is Bond" – this album has something for everybody. The chilled-out album opener "The Iceberg", the dope 9-minute posse cut "What Ya Wanna Do", the personal "This One's For Me", the gangster tale "Peel Their Caps Back", the thought-provoking "You Played Yourself", the multi-layered noise on "The Hunted Child" and "Lethal Weapon" – this album is packed with dope tracks. The album's most important theme – as evidenced in the album's subtitle and the song "Freedom Of Speech" – is the PMRC censorship that was being imposed on Hip-Hop artists at the time.

The Iceberg/Freedom of Speech… Just Watch What You Say! is a tight album, one of Ice T's best and the one that established Ice-T as one of Hip Hop's most prominent personalities.

Top tracks: You Played Yourself | This One's On Me | The Hunted Child | Lethal Weapon

32. Big Daddy Kane - It's A Big Daddy Thing (1989)

"Come, get some, you little bum / I take the cake but you can't get a crumb / From the poetic, authentic, superior / Ultimate – and all that good shit" (Warm It Up)

Maybe not as groundbreaking as his debut 'Long Live the Kane', still this album shows Big Daddy Kane in top form.

This album is a just a little too long (with a few filler tracks) to be considered a true classic, but BDK's persona and lyrical ability throughout make this an essential Golden Age album.

Top tracks: Another Victory | Mortal Combat | Warm It Up | Smooth Operator

33. Schoolly D - Schoolly D (1985)

"PSK we're making that green / People always say, "What the hell does that mean?"..." (P.S.K. What Does It Mean)

Often recognized as the first 'gangster rapper', Schoolly D dropped an underground classic with this debut. Hard-ass beats & lyrics: vintage Schoolly D.

Top tracks: P.S.K. What Does It Mean | Gucci Time | I Don't Like Rock & Roll | Freestyle Rappin'

34. Marley Marl - In Control Vol 1 (1988)

"Yo, Marley gives the slice, I get nice / And my voice is twice as horrifying as Vincent Price" (The Symphony)

With the Juice Crew and it's individual members in full effect, 1988 was also the year for this Marley Marl compilation album. An album filled with dope tracks, with the standout "The Symphony" as its biggest attraction.

Top tracks: The Symphony | Droppin' Science | Simon Says | Live Motivator

35. Biz Markie - Goin Off (1988)

"Can you feel it / Nothin' can save ya / For this is the season of catchin' the vapors" (Vapors)

Another Marley Marl production from the Juice Crew golden era. Biz Markie always was the joker character from that group of artists – originally a beatboxer, but a decent emcee. Nothing deep here, just funny rhymes and Biz' antics over Marley's dope beats.

Top tracks: Goin' Off | Nobody Beats The Biz | Make The Music With Your Mouth, Biz | Vapors

36. Too Short - Life Is… (1988)

"I remember how it all began / I used to sing dirty raps to my East Side fans" (Life Is… Too Short)

My favorite Too Short album from his extensive discography. Already a Hip-Hop veteran in 1988, Too Short came into his own on this album. Trademark explicit lyrics, with his typical laid back flow and music to ride to. This album is one of his most consistent ones and contains a few classic tracks. A West Coast classic.

Top tracks: Life Is… | Cusswords | I Ain't Trippin' | Nobody Does It Better

37. LL Cool J - Walking With A Panther (1989)

I release the juice smack dab in your face / Do damage, I'm pickin' up the pace / My mics' like a torch when I'm walkin' at nighttime / straight to the dome, it's like a pipeline" (It Gets No Rougher)

LL Cool J's much maligned third album. It got slammed because it contains two or three (admittedly pretty bad) love songs, but the album is long enough and dope enough to bypass that BS. 15 dope tracks is more than enough to make this an album to be respected and loved.

Top tracks: It Gets No Rougher | Droppin 'Em | Going Back To Cali | Fast Peg

38. MC Shan - Down By The Law (1987)

"Hip Hop was set out in the dark, they used to do it out in the park" (The Bridge)

A very solid debut by MC Shan. You can't go wrong with Marley Marl on the boards. Tracks like 'The Bridge' & 'Kill That Noise' sparked the bridge wars between the Juice Crew and Boogie Down Productions, and although BDP emerged victorious, MC Shan more than held his own & the Juice Crew's on this one.

Top tracks: The Bridge | Kill That Noise | Down By Law | Living In The World Of Hip Hop

39. Run DMC - Tougher Than Leather (1988)

"Some underestimate / And miscalculate / My intent to create what I call the great" (Run's House)

By 1988, Run DMC were no longer solo king-of-the-hill in Hip Hop. Also, they faced the impossible task following up their mega successful third album, the 1986 classic 'Raising Hell.' They pretty much succeeded with Tougher

Than Leather. Typical Run DMC: high energy, braggadocios, hard-hitting but clean – some say it was their last great one.

Top tracks: Run's House | Beats To The Rhyme | Mary Mary | I'm Not Going Out Like That

40. 3rd Bass - The Cactus Album (1989)

"Ready in the intro, cue up the Serch-lite / Point us to the center stage, I'll grab the first mic / Projectin' the voice with this mic that I'm cuffin' / You ain't my nucka, sucker I'm snuffin'" (Steppin' to the A.M.)

A long, but excellent album. It could have done without the skits, but it is pretty much dope form start to finish. MC Serch & Pete Nice are competent emcees and the production & beats are excellent. Essential Golden Age material. Also notable for the first appearance of MF DOOM (as KMD's Zev Love X)

Top tracks: Brooklyn-Queens | The Gas Face | Triple Stage Darkness | Steppin' to the A.M.

41. DJ Jazzy Jeff & The Fresh Prince - He's The DJ I'm The Rapper (1988)

"It's new, it's out of the ordinary / It's rather extraordinary, so yo bust this commentary / A literary genius and a superior beat creator / Have come together, and we made a / Musical composition which we think is a remedy / To cure all the dance floors that's empty..." (Brand New Funk)

He's The DJ, I'm The Rapper was the duo's second album and the first double in Hip Hop. It was a huge success, reaching triple platinum status. It established pioneering DJ Jazzy Jeff as one of the all-time great DJs in Hip Hop and was the stepping stone to Will Smith's international superstar status. Back then, The Fresh Prince was a talented emcee with a dope flow and great story telling skills. Together, they were one of the acts responsible for making Hip Hop accessible to a wider audience, when it was still cool to create clean and fun Hip Hop music.

Top tracks: As We Go | Here We Go Again | Brand New Funk | Time To Chill

42. Run DMC - King Of Rock (1985)

"I'm the king of rock, there is none higher / Sucker MC's should call me sire / To burn my kingdom, you must use fire / I won't stop rockin' till I retire" (King Of Rock)

Run DMC's second album established them as Hip Hop's top act of the time and was the stepping stone to one of Hip Hop's biggest albums ever: Raising Hell.

Top tracks: King Of Rock | Darryl And Joe | Jam Master Jammin | Can You Rock It Like This

43. Gang Starr - No More Mr. Nice Guy (1989)

"I suggest you take a breath for the words I manifest, they will scold you and mold you, while I impress upon you the fact

that, I use my tact at rhymin for climbin, and chill while I attract that girl you're with..." (Manifest)

Gang Starr's debut album. They were coming into their sound here, which setup the albums - Step In The Arena and Daily Operation. This is a dope album in its own right and a must-have for any Gang Starr fan.

Top tracks: Manifest | Conscience Be Free | DJ Premier In Deep Concentration | Positivity

44. Mantronix - Mantronix (1985)

"We're back, we're fresh and were here to stay..." (Bassline)

Producer Kurtis Mantronik did some classic work in the 1980s, producing for the likes of Just Ice and T la Rock. He also dropped a few dope 'electronic' Hip Hop albums as a duo with MC Tee, with this 1985 debut album being their best.

Top tracks: Needle To The Groove | Bassline | Ladies | Hardcore Hip Hop

45. MC Lyte - Eyes On This (1989)

"You can cha-cha-cha to this Mardis Gras / I'm the dopest female that you've heard thus far" (Cha Cha Cha)

MC Lyte second album establishes her as one of the best emcees out there, male or female. With Lyte on the mic and production from EPMD's Parrish Smith, Brand

Nubian's Grand Puba, Audio Two & Marley Marl, you can't go wrong with this album.

Top tracks: Cha Cha Cha | Cappucino | Shut the Eff Up! (Hoe) | Not Wit' A Dealer

46. Jungle Brothers - Done By the Forces Of Nature (1989)

"Round and round, upside down / Living my life underneath the ground / Never heard of and hardly seen / A whole lot of talk about the Red, Black and Green" (Beyond This World)

The Jungle Brothers never received the same recognition their fellow Native Tongues crews De La Soul, and A Tribe Called Quest did, but their first two albums are straight up Native Tongue classics. Their 1988 debut Straight Out Of The Jungle is a classic, this one is more than a worthy follow-up. Conscious, positive and funky – what's not to like?

Top tracks: Doin' Our Own Dang | Beyond This World | Sunshine | What U Waitin' 4

47. Whodini - Escape (1984)

"Friends / Is a word we use every day / Most the time we use it in the wrong way / Now you can look the word up, again and again / But the dictionary doesn't know the meaning of friends…" (Friends)

Whodini are pioneers in the Hip Hop game who never got the recognition they truly deserved. This is their dopest album. Straight positive and full of messaging. Listen to it nowadays and you'll see what I'm sayin'.

Top tracks: Five Minutes Of Funk | Friends | Freaks Come Out A Night | Escape

48. Low Profile - We're In This Together (1989)

"Mic check, now in effect / Suckers still comin short / That's why I'm callin order in the court / It looks like a lotta suckers gotta learn the hard way / It doesn't pay when you tamper with my deejay" (Aladdin's On A Rampage)

Low Profile is a collaboration between World Champion DJ Aladdin and rapper WC before he formed WC & The MAAD Circle. This album is a real Hip Hop album; with a WC on the mic before he started gangster rap and a DJ with dope turntable techniques. Consistent throughout, this is a slept on West Coast classic.

Top tracks: Aladdin's On A Rampage | How Ya Livin' | Pay Ya Dues | Keep Em Flowi

49. Nice & Smooth - Nice & Smooth (1989)

"Rap czar, superstar / No limitation in my life and I'm known to go far" (Early To Rise)

Another forgotten classic from a time when it was still OK to make humorous, clean and catchy Hip Hop. One of Hip Hop most respected duo's, this was their signature album and their best, perhaps.

Top tracks: Funky For You | No Delayin' | Ooh Child | Early To Rise

50. DJ Jazzy Jeff & The Fresh Prince - Rock The House (1987)

"Well, it's true that I'm the reigning king of the throne / But with all my strength, I couldn't do it alone / I need a deejay like (Jazzy) to back me up / So when I'm rockin on the mic he's on the crossfade cut" (The Magnificent Jazzy Jeff)

Two kids from Philly – a dope emcee with great flow and storytelling abilities and an awesome DJ. Their talents were already obvious on this debut record. The Fresh Prince would grow up to be an international (movie) star, and Jazzy Jeff into one of the most hailed DJs in Hip Hop ever. This is a great debut, with some classic tracks, in an era when it was OK for Hip Hop to be fun.

Top Tracks: The Magnificent Jazzy Jeff | Rock The House | Just One Of Those Days | Girls Are Nothing But Trouble

51. Wild Style Soundtrack (1983)

52. Chill Rob G – Ride The Rhythm (1989)

53. Just Ice – Back To The Old School (1986)

54. Dana Dane – Dana Dane With Fame (1987)

55. Doug E Fresh – Oh My God (1986)

56. Superlover Cee & Casanova Rud – Girls I Got Em Locked (1988)

VOLUME TWO

57. Young MC – Stone Cold Rhymin (1989)

58. Treacherous Three – Treacherous Three (1984)

59. Stetsasonic – In Full Gear (1988)

60. Kool Moe Dee – How Ya Like Me Know (1987)

61. Grandmaster Melle Mel – Piano (1989)

62. King Tee – Act A Fool (1988)

63. Fat Boys – Fat Boys (1984)

64. UTFO – UTFO (1985)

65. Afrika Bambaataa – Planet Rock (1986)

66. MC Shan – Born To Be Wild (1988)

67. Salt N Pepa – Hot Cool & Vicious (1986)

68. Schoolly D – Am I Black Enough For You? (1989)

69. Too Short – Born To Mack (1987)

70. Awesome Dre – You Can't Hold Me Back (1989)

71. Lakim Shabazz – Pure Righteousness (1988)

72. Tuff Crew – Back To Wreck Shop (1989)

73. Skinny Boys – Weightless (1986)

74. Special Ed – Youngest In Charge (1989)

75. DJ Cash Money & Marvelous – Where's The Party At? (1988)

76. Kool Moe Dee – Kool Moe Dee (1986)

77. Queen Latifah – All Hail The Queen (1989)

78. Kurtis Blow – Kurtis Blow (1980)

79. The 7A3 – Coolin In Cali (1988)

80. Just Ice – Kool And Deadly (1987)

81. Rhyme Syndicate – Comin' Through (1988)

82. Kwame The Boy Genius – Featuring A New Beginning (1989)

83. 2 Live Crew – 2 Live Is What We Are (1986)

84. Whodini – Back In Black (1986)

85. T la Rock – Lyrical King (1987)

86. Three Times Dope – Original Stylin' (1989)

87. Tuff Crew – Danger Zone (1988)

88. Mantronix – Music Madness (1986)

89. Skinny Boys – Skinny & Proud (1987)

90. JVC Force – Doin Damage (1988)

91. Fat Boys – The Fat Boys Are Back (1985)

92. Steady B – Bring The Beat Back (1986)

93. Donald D – Notorious (1989)

94. Heavy D & The Boyz – Livin' Large (1987)

95. Schoolly D – Smoke Some Kill (1988)

96. Willie Dee – Controversy (1989)

97. Doug E Fresh – The World's Greatest Entertainer (1988)

98. Stezo – Crazy Noise (1989)

99. Kid N Play – 2 Hype (1988)

100. Masters Of Ceremony – Dynamite (1988)

1980

The Godfather of Rap "Kurtis Blow" on Soul Train

Rap music gained further momentum when one of their star musicians, Kurtis Blow, performed on Soul Train. Soul Train was aired on TV, and Kurtis was a hit. He became the very first rap artist to appear and perform on the weekly syndicated, R&B and soul-leaning, music program, Soul Train. As the tide was turning and rap music was starting to gain momentum, host Don Cornelius begrudgingly invited Blow to perform his unstoppable hit single "The Breaks," which was riding high on sales charts at the time. During the interview segment, Cornelius admitted to Kurtis Blow that he didn't really get the attraction to this new style of music that was emerging but, nonetheless, continued to feature hip-hop artists on the program as the genre continued to get bigger. Kurt Walker has a number of claims on the history of hip-hop. Under the moniker Kurtis Blow, he was the first rapper to sign to a major label, Mercury. He was the first to embark on a national tour and was also the first rapper to appear on network television, performing 'The Breaks.' Built around a series of disco breaks, but also bemoaning the bad luck a person can have in love, Kurtis Blow's Soul Train show (in suit jacket with nothing underneath) helped to catapult 'The Breaks' to gold record status – another first.

Kurtis Blow's First Album

'Kurtis Blow' - the self-entitled album of "the Godfather of Rap, Kurtis Blow" was released in 1980 by Mercury Records. The record includes the song "The Breaks", which was often sampled later in hip-hop records, mainly for its introduction made by Blow's a cappella vocal, and for the drum break, giving a wordplay dimension to the title. "Rappin' Blow, Pt. 2" was issued as a single that had a do-it-yourself B-side, the instrumental version. "Takin' Care of Business" is one of the first hip hop and rock 'n' roll crossover attempts.

TRACKS

Side One:

"Rappin' Blow, Pt. 2"

"The Breaks"

"Way Out West"

Side Two:

"Throughout Your Years"

"Hard Times"

"All I Want in This World (Is to Find That Girl)"

"Takin' Care of Business"

CD bonus tracks:

"Christmas Rappin'"

"Breaks [Instrumental]"

Personnel

Musicians:

Vocals: Kurtis Blow, Sudana Bobatoon, Wayne Garfield, Sheila Spencer, William Waring, Adam White

Guitars: Eddie Martinez, J.B. Moore, Dean Swenson, John Tropea

Keyboards: Onaje Allen Gumbs, J.B. Moore

Bass: Craig Short, Tom Wolk

Drums: Jimmy Bralower

Production

Produced By Robert Ford & J.B. Moore

Engineers: Rod Hui

Assistant Engineers: Erik Block, Paula Stevens, Lisa Zimet

Mixing: Vincent Davis

Mastering: Suha Gur

Sugarhill Gang's Album Release

The album was released in 1980 for Sugarhill Records and was produced by Sylvia Robinson. The single "Rapper's Delight" was a #36 hit on the US pop chart and a #4 hit on the R&B chart. Although "Rapper's Delight" was the only charting single, the album also included the minor hit, "Rapper's Reprise". The remainder of the LP consists several down-tempo soul tracks and a disco instrumental, as Sylvia Robinson didn't believe an album consisting entirely of hip hop music would be commercially viable in 1980.

TRACKS

"Here I Am"

"Rapper's Reprise (Jam, Jam)" featuring The Sequence

"Bad News Don't Bother Me"

"Sugarhill Groove"

"Passion Play"

"Rapper's Delight" [shortened single version]

Personnel

Rappers – Big Bank Hank, Master Gee, Wonder Mike (The Sugarhill Gang)

Backing Vocals, and Rhythm Arrangements – Positive Force (tracks 3, 5, 6)

Bass – Bernard Rowland (tracks 3, 5, 6), Douglas Wimbish, possibly Chip Shearin (track 6)

Drums – Bryan Horton (tracks 3, 5, 6), Keith LeBlanc

Guitar – Albert Pittman (tracks 3, 5, 6), Skip McDonald, possibly Brian Morgan (track 6)

Keyboards – Nate Edmonds, Skitch Smith

Percussion – Craig Derry, Harry Reyes, John Stump

Vibraphone, Backing Vocals – Sylvia Robinson

Special Guest Appearance – Tito Puente

Special Effects – Billy Jones, Nate Edmonds

Producer, Engineer, Mixed By – Billy Jones, Nate Edmonds, Sylvia Robinson

'Zulu Nation's Throwdown'

In 1980, Taylor's groups made Death Mix, their first recording with Paul Winley Records. According to Bambaata, this was an unauthorized release. Winley recorded two versions of Soulsonic Force's landmark single, "Zulu Nation Throwdown," with authorization from the musicians. Disappointed with the results of the single, Bambaataa left the company. The arranger credit on these recordings is correctly attributed to Harlem Underground Band leader, Kevin Donovan. This led to the false assumption that Bambaataa's real name was Kevin Donovan, which was widely accepted by the hip hop community until recently, following sexual abuse allegations, when Bronx River residents spoke out and revealed in oral testimonies that Bambaataa's real name was in fact Lance Taylor. The Zulu Nation was the first hip-hop organization, with an official birth date of November 12, 1977. Bambaataa's plan with the Universal Zulu Nation was to build a movement out of the creativity of a new generation of outcast youths with an authentic, liberating worldview.

1981

Rap Music on NBC

A new group called The Funky 4 plus One More was invited to play for NBC's Saturday Night Live show. They perform their hit song "That's The Joint." Funky 4 + 1 was an American hip hop group from The Bronx, New York. The instrumental track, carried by Sugarhill bassist Doug Wimbish, is so compelling that for a while I listened to it alone on its B-side version. And the rapping is the peak of the form, not verbally—the debut has funnier words—but rhythmically. Quick tradeoffs and clamorous breaks vary the steady-flow rhyming of the individual MCs, and when it comes to Sha-Rock, Miss Plus One herself, who needs variation?" They were the first hip hop group to appear on a national television show; on February 14 (Valentine's Day) 1981 they performed in Saturday Night Live hosted by Blondie's Deborah Harry. The group was subsequently asked by Harry to open up for Blondie on tour, but were forbidden to do so by Sugarhill Records' CEO, Sylvia Robinson.

Members of the group:

The Voice of K.K. aka K.K. Rockwell (Kevin Smith)

Keith Keith (Keith Caesar)

Sha Rock (Sharon Green)

Rahiem (Guy Todd Williams)

Lil' Rodney C! (Rodney Stone)

Jazzy Jeff (Jeff Miree)

D.J. Breakout (Keith Williams)

D.J. Baron (Baron Chappell)

Kurtis Blow's Second Album Release

'Deuce' is Kurtis Blow's second album, released in 1981. It peaked at #35 on the R&B charts, and #137 on the Billboard 200.

TRACKS

"Deuce"

"It's Gettin' Hot"

"Getaway"

"Starlife"

"Take It to the Bridge"

"Do the Do"

"Rockin"

Blondie's "Rapture" - First "Rap" Video Played on MTV

What happens when a punk band trying to spice up its repertoire attempts to do so by adopting what New York City punk bands—let alone pop culture—rarely ventured to for its hits? You get the first rap video on MTV, in MTV's first month on the air, in their first 90-video rotation, which arrived in the form of Blondie's "Rapture," the entire coda of which is rapped by Debbie Harry. To hammer the point home, Blondie also recruited hip-hop luminaries to appear in the video with them, like Fab Five Freddy (who's name-checked in the song), Lee Quinones, and Jean-Michel Basquiat.

"Rapture" came at a weirdly perfect time as it wasn't just the first video featuring rap on MTV, but was a video in MTV's first real "rotation," where it stayed for a few months. In other words, eyes from all over the country saw this young white woman doing the "hip-hop" thing. At the time, it was neither an abomination nor a momentous occasion, but just a weird rock thing that was, if not amusing, then actually fairly cool. The video helped cement Blondie's place as one of the more progressive bands in contemporary rock, and set the precedent for rock embracing hip-hop (and vice-versa).

8th Wonder released by The Sugarhill Gang

The Sugarhill Gang is an American hip hop group. 8th Wonder is the second album by rap group The Sugarhill Gang. The album was released in 1981 for Sugar Hill Records and was once again produced by Sylvia Robinson and James Cullimore. Though not as successful as the group's previous album, the album did feature the minor hits "8th Wonder" and "Apache" and featured an appearance by another Sugar Hill Records rap group, Grandmaster Flash and the Furious Five on "Showdown".

TRACKS

"Funk Box"

"On the Money"

"8th Wonder"

"Apache"

"Showdown" (featuring Grandmaster Flash and the Furious Five)

"Giggalo"

"Hot Hot Summer Day"

Beastie Boys

The Beastie Boys are an hip-hop group from New York City formed in 1981. The group comprised of Michael "Mike D" Diamond (vocals, drums), Adam "MCA" Yauch (vocals, bass) and Adam "Ad-Rock" Horovitz (vocals, guitar). The Beastie Boys were formed as a four-piece hardcore punk band, the Young Aborigines, in 1979 by Mike D (vocals), MCA (bass), John Berry (guitar) and Kate Schellenbach (drums). They appeared on the compilation cassette New York Thrash, contributing two songs from their first EP, Polly Wog Stew, in 1982. Berry left shortly thereafter and was replaced by Horovitz. After achieving local success with the 1983 experimental hip hop single "Cooky Puss", the Beastie Boys made a full transition to hip hop, and Schellenbach left the group soon after. They toured with Madonna in 1985 and a year later released their debut album Licensed to Ill. It was followed by Paul's Boutique, Check Your Head, Ill Communication, Hello Nasty, and Hot Sauce Committee Part Two. The Beastie Boys have sold 26 million records in the United States and 50 million records worldwide, making them the biggest-selling rap group since Billboard began recording sales in 1991. With seven platinum-selling albums from 1986 to 2004, the Beastie Boys were one of the longest-lived hip hop acts worldwide.

Prior to forming the Beastie Boys, Michael Diamond was part of a number of bands such as the Walden Jazz Band, BAN, and The Young Aborigines. The Beastie Boys formed in July 1981 when the Young Aborigines bassist Jeremy Shatan left New York City for the summer and the remaining members Michael Diamond, John Berry and Kate Schellenbach formed a new hardcore punk band with Adam Yauch called Beastie Boys. In an interview on The Tonight Show in October 2018, Mike D stated that the Beastie name is an acronym. It stands for "Boys Entering Anarchistic States Towards Inner Excellence". The band supported Bad Brains, the Dead Kennedys, the Misfits and Reagan Youth at venues such as CBGB, A7, Trudy Hellers Place and Max's Kansas City, playing at the latter venue on its closing night. In November 1982, the Beastie Boys recorded the 7" EP Polly Wog Stew at 171A studios, an early recorded example of New York hardcore.

1982

GRANDMASTER FLASH AND THE FURIOUS FIVE'S DEBUT ALBUM

'The Message' was released in October 1982 by Sugar Hill Records. It features the influential eponymous track and hip-hop single "The Message". It was the only album released while the group's original line-up was together. The album charted at number 53 in the United States and at number 77 in the United Kingdom. It was ranked as the 21st best album of 1982 in Robert Christgau's list for the Pazz & Jop critics' poll. In Christgau's Record Guide: The '80s (1990), he gave the album an A-minus and said, although "She's Fresh" is the "only instant killer", each song's attempt to experiment and "touch a lot of bases with a broad demographic ... justifies itself".

In a retrospective review, AllMusic's Ron Wynn gave The

Message four-and-a-half out of five stars and called it the group's "ultimate peak" whose highlight was the title track. Miles Marshall Lewis, writing in The Rolling Stone Album Guide (2004), gave its 2002 British reissue four out of five stars and cited "The Adventures of Grandmaster Flash on the Wheels of Steel" as the album's "clincher" and "the only prime-period example of Flash's ability to set and shatter moods, with his turntables and faders running through a collage of at least 10 records that sound like hundreds." Colin Larkin also gave it four stars in his Encyclopedia of Popular Music (2006). Mark Richardson from Pitchfork said The Message featured "two absolutely essential songs"—the title track and "Scorpio," which he dubbed "the greatest early electro track." However, he felt the rest of the songs were inferior and gave the album a score of 6.4 out of 10. The album was also included in the book 1001 Albums You Must Hear Before You Die.

TRACKS

"She's Fresh"

"It's Nasty"

"Scorpio"

"It's a Shame (Mt. Airy Groove)"

"Dreamin'"

"You Are"

"The Message"

Kurtis Blow releases Third Album

'Tough' is the third album by rapper Kurtis Blow, released in 1982 on Mercury Records. It reached #38 on the Black Albums chart and #167 on the Pop Albums charts. The single "Tough" reached #37 on the Black Singles chart.

TRACKS

"Tough"

"Juice"

"Daydreamin'"

"Boogie Blues"

"Baby You've Got to Go"

First Hip Hop International Tour

In 1982, Bambaataa and his followers - a group of dancers, artists, and DJs - went outside the United States on the first hip-hop tour. He saw that the hip hop tours would be the key to help expand hip hop and his Universal Zulu Nation. In addition it would help promote the values of hip hop that he believed are based on peace, unity, love, and having fun. He brought peace to the gangs; many artists and gang members say that "hip hop saved a lot of lives." His influence inspired many overseas artists like the French rapper MC Solaar. He was a popular DJ in The South Bronx rap scene and became known not only as Afrika Bambaataa but also as the "Master of Records." He established two rap crews: the Jazzy 5 including MCs Master Ice, Mr. Freeze, Master Bee, Master D.E.E, and AJ Les, and the second crew referred to as Soulsonic Force including Mr. Biggs, Pow Wow and Emcee G.L.O.B.E.

In 1982, Taylor, who was inspired by Kraftwerk's futuristic electronic music, debuted at The Roxy a test cassette of EBN-OZN's ground breaking, 12-inch white rap/spoken word "AEIOU Sometimes Y". It was the first commercially released American single ever made on a computer, a Fairlight CMI, ushering in the era of music computer sampling. In that same year, Bambaataa and Soulsonic Force dropped the live band to go high-tech. Bambaataa credited the pioneering Japanese electro-pop group, Yellow Magic Orchestra, whose work he sampled, as an inspiration. He also borrowed a keyboard hook from German electronic pioneers Kraftwerk and was provided the electronic Roland TR-808 "beat-box" by producer Arthur Baker and synthesizer player John Robie. That resulted in "Planet Rock," which went to gold status and generated an entire school of "electro-boogie" rap and dance music. Bambaataa formed his own label to release the Time Zone Compilation. He created "turntablism" as its own subgenre and the ratification of "electronica" as an industry-certified trend in the late 1990s.

Wild Style is released

Wild Style is an American hip-hop film produced by Charlie Ahearn. Released theatrically in September 1982 by First Run Features and later re-released for home video by Rhino Home Video, it is regarded as the first hip hop motion picture. The film included seminal figures within the given period, such as Fab Five Freddy, Lee Quiñones, Lady Pink, The Rock Steady Crew, The Cold Crush Brothers, Queen Lisa Lee of Zulu Nation, Grandmaster Flash and Zephyr. The protagonist "Zoro" is played by New York graffiti artist "Lee" George Quiñones.

An early version of the Wild Style logo appeared in 1981 when Charlie Ahearn hired graffiti writer Dondi to paint the 'window down' subway car piece that appears in the film. The Dondi piece was the inspiration for the animated title sequence designed by the artist, Zephyr in 1982. The Wild Style mural was painted by Zephyr, Revolt and Sharp in 1983. Charlie Ahearn and Fab 5 Freddy began working on the film on late 1981. The approach was a hybrid of a narrative musical and documentary, having the real hip hop pioneers play themselves in a loosely scripted story shot entirely in the South Bronx, the Lower East Side and MTA subway yards.

Wild Style takes place in 1981 in New York and centers around graffiti artists, Zoro (played by Lee Quiñones) and his encounters with an uptown journalist named, Virginia (played by Patti Astor). More so than its story, however, the film is notable for featuring several prominent figures from early hip hop culture such as Busy Bee Starski, Fab Five Freddy, The Cold Crush Brothers and Grandmaster Flash. Throughout the movie there are scenes depicting activities common in the early days of hip hop. These include MCing, turntablism, graffiti and b-boying. The film demonstrates the interconnections between music, dance and art in the development of hip hop culture.

1983

KDAY Hires Greg Mack (and Becomes America's First True Hip-Hop Radio Station)

Other stations had played rap before KDAY, but it wasn't until the hiring of Greg "Mack" Macmillan as their program director and afternoon host that everything changed. Mack turned the station into a hip-hop powerhouse, recruiting young talent to not only to DJ, but to have their ears to the streets. One such talent pool? The World Class Wreckin' Cru, whose Dr. Dre had started to mix tracks together on a mixer in real time, splicing old tracks into contemporary rap records.

The station became one of the most influential outlets for rap nearly overnight, and broke some of the most important records in the history of rap. Moreover, it created the market for rap radio formats, and if hot rap singles begin anywhere, it's on rap format radio. KDAY would eventually turn over from a rap format station in 1991, and would relaunch as a less-influential version of the original in 2004 as a middle-ground urban contemporary station. More importantly, however, KDAY lead terrestrial radio executives to realize that the rap format would be a crucial one in years to come, spawning the creation of rap radio all over America.

PBS Airs Style Wars

In 1983, as hip-hop culture continued its ascent into the mainstream culture, piquing the curiosity of the public, PBS aired a then-little known documentary about graffiti, break dancing, and hip-hop culture titled Style Wars. The film—one of the first real looks into hip-hop as it was happening in New York City—wasn't a smash ratings hit or a definitive moment for PBS, or even hip-hop. Its due credit would come with its legacy. In the short term, however, it did make the Rock Steady Crew, and artists like Dondi, Seen, Kase 2 and more into household names, at least for the households who saw it.

The movie lives in infamy as one of the most critically acclaimed films, not just about graffiti culture and its place in hip-hop, but an art form still very much on the rise, the likes of which very little else exists. It's one of the great documentaries of the '80s. It would be the first line in co-director Tony Silver's obituary, and in the obituaries of several of its "stars." In 2011, an effort to restore some of the old footage that wasn't used in the film started as a grassroots campaign by co-director Henry Chalfant, and eventually met its goal via crowdfunding site Kickstarter.

British impresario 'Malcolm McLaren' Album Release

'Duck Rock' is an album released by British impresario Malcolm McLaren. It was originally issued in 1983 by Charisma Records, Virgin Records, and Chrysalis Records, and later re-released on CD in 1987. The album mixes up styles from South Africa, Central and South America, the Caribbean, and the United States, including hip hop. The album proved to be highly influential in bringing hip hop to a wider audience in the United Kingdom. Two of the singles from the album, "Buffalo Gals" and "Double Dutch", became major chart hits on both sides of the Atlantic. Duck Rock was dedicated to Harry McClintock, better known as Haywire Mac. The album artwork was designed by Dondi White and Nick Egan, with the illustration by Keith Haring.

TRACKS

Side One:

"Obatala (La Republica Dominicana)"

"Buffalo Gals"

"Double Dutch"

"El San Juanera"

"Merengue"

"Punk It Up"

Side Two:

"Legba"

"Jive My Baby"

"Song for Chango"

"(Living on the Road In) Soweto"

"World's Famous"

"Duck for the Oyster"

Wild Style Original Soundtrack was released

The official soundtrack to the 1983 hip hop film 'Wild Style' was originally released in 1983 via Animal Records, and re-released twice: in 1997 via Rhino Entertainment, and in 2007 as 25th anniversary edition via Mr. Bongo

Records. The album was produced by Charlie Ahearn and Chris Stein with Fab 5 Freddy, who served as musical director of the project. It featured appearances from Busy Bee, Cold Crush Brothers, DJ Charlie Chase, Grandmaster Caz, Grand Mixer DXT, Grand Wizzard Theodore & the Fantastic Five, Double Trouble (Rodney Cee & Kevie Kev Rockwell of Funky 4 + 1), Prince Whipper Whip, Rammellzee, AJ Scratch, D.J. Stieve Steve and Shockdell.

TRACKS

Disc One:

Military Cut – Scratch Mix- DJ Grand Wizard Theodore

M.C. Battle – Busy Bee Vs. Rodney Cee

Basketball Throwdown – Cold Crush Brothers Vs. Fantastic Freaks

Fantastic Freaks at the Dixie - Fantastic Freaks

Subway Theme – Scratch Mix by Grand Wizard Theodore, Chris Stein (Previously Unreleased)

Cold Crush Brothers at the Dixie – Cold Crush Brothers

Busy Bee's Limo Rap – Busy Bee

Cuckoo Clocking - Fab 5 Freddy (previously unreleased)

Stoop Rap – Rodney Cee & KK Rockwell aka Double Trouble

Double Trouble at the Amphitheatre – Double Trouble

South Bronx Subway Rap – Grandmaster Caz, Chris Stein (Original Version)

Street Rap by Busy Bee – Busy Bee (Previously Unreleased)

Busy Bee at the Amphitheatre – Busy Bee

Fantastic Freaks at the Amphitheatre - Fantastic Freaks

Gangbusters – Scratch Mix by Grand Wizard Theodore

Rammellzee & Shock Dell at the Amphitheatre – Rammellzee & Shock Dell

Down By Law – Fab 5 Freddy & Chris Stein (Previously Unreleased) 25th Anniversary Edition

Disc Two:

Wildstyle Lesson - Kev Luckhurst aka Phat Kev

Limousine Rap (Crime Don't Pay Mix) - Wild Style Allstars

Basketball Throwdown (Dixie: Razorcut Mix) Cold Crush Brothers vs. Fantastic Freaks

Stoop Rap (LP Version South Bronx Mix) - Double Trouble

Street Rap (Subway Mix) - Busy Bee

Stoop Rap (Film Version) Double Trouble

B Boy Beat (Instrumental) - Wild Style Allstars

Yawning Beat (Instrumental) - Wild Style Allstars

Crime Cut (Instrumental) - Wild Style Allstars

Gangbusters (Instrumental) - DJ Grand Wizard Theodore

Cuckoo Clocking (Instrumental) - Fab 5 Freddy

Meetings (Instrumental) - Wild Style Allstars

Military Cut (Instrumental) - DJ Grand Wizard Theodore

Razor Cut (Instrumental) - Wild Style Allstars

Subway Theme (Instrumental) - DJ Grand Wizard Theodore, Chris Stein

Busy Bees (Instrumental) - Busy Bee

Down By Law (Instrumental) - Fab 5 Freddy

Baby Beat (Instrumental) - Wild Style Allstars

Jungle Beat (Instrumental) - Wild Style Allstars

Wild Style Scratch Tool - Kev Luckhurst aka Phat Kev

Kurtis Blow releases 4th album

Party Time? is an LP by rapper Kurtis Blow, released in 1983 on Mercury Records. The title track and the song

"Got to Dance" were both party-themed, but the other songs struck a sociopolitical tone.

TRACKS

"Party Time"

"Big Time Hood"

"Nervous"

"Got to Dance"

"One-Two-Five (Main Street, Harlem, USA)"

'Whodini' was released by Whodini

'Whodini' is the self-titled debut album by the hip-hop group Whodini. It was released in 1983 via Jive Records and spawned two hit singles: "Magic's Wand" and "The Haunted House of Rock". Audio production was handled by Conny Plank, Heatwave's Roy Carter, Thomas Dolby, and the Willesden Dodgers (Nigel Green, Pete Q. Harris, Richard Joh Smith).

Grandmaster Flash sues Sugarhill Records for $5 million

Grandmaster Flash and the Furious Five initially built their reputation performing at parties and live shows in the late 1970s and achieved local success. By the time the Sugarhill Gang's "Rapper's Delight" was released, the group realized the potential of cutting records and signed with various labels until staying with Sugar Hill Records. Under Sugar Hill Records, the group rose to prominence in the early 1980s with their first hit "Freedom" (1980). It was not until the release of "The Message" (1982) and the album of the same name that they achieved mainstream success.

In 1983, Grandmaster Flash, who never appeared on any of the group's studio recordings, sued Sugar Hill Records for $5 million in unpaid royalties. This resulted in the single "White Lines (Don't Don't Do It)" being credited to "Grandmaster & Melle Mel". The song reached #47 in Billboard's Hot R&B/Hip-Hop Songs chart. Another lawsuit was filed over certain elements of the song being stolen from "Cavern" by Liquid Liquid, from which Sugar Hill Records would never recover. The royalties dispute split the group, and Melle Mel left, soon followed by Mr. Ness/Scorpio and Cowboy after "White Lines (Don't Don't Do It)" was a hit, where they formed Grandmaster Melle Mel and the Furious Five and released the album Grandmaster Melle Mel and the Furious Five in 1984. Meanwhile, Grandmaster Flash, The Kidd Creole, and Rahiem left for Elektra Records and included to the group three new members "The Lord LaVon" (Kevin L. Dukes – Phenomenal writer, Rapper and Bassist), Russell Wheeler (Rapper – "Mr. Broadway") and "Larry-Love" (Larry

Parker – Dancer). They worked under the name "Grandmaster Flash" on They Said It Couldn't Be Done, The Source, and Ba-Dop-Boom-Bang.

The additional members The Lord La Von, Larry Love and Mr. Broadway formed the "Furious Five" but they could not use the name as Sugar Hill Records owned the rights. Grandmaster Flash and his new "Furious Five" had hits with their three albums, which made it to the top fifty of Billboard's R&B/Hip-Hop Albums chart, whereas Melle Mel and his group fared better, most notably with the recording of "Beat Street Breakdown", which peaked at #8 in the R&B chart. During this period, Melle Mel gained higher success, appearing in Chaka Khan's "I Feel for You", which won the Grammy Award for Best Female R&B Vocal Performance in 1985.

Melle Mel's Debut Song Release

White Lines (Don't Don't Do It)" is a song by hip-hop legend, Melle Mel, released as a 12-inch single in 1983 on Sugar Hill Records. The song, which warns against the dangers of cocaine, addiction, and drug smuggling, is one of Melle Mel's signature tracks. The bassline is taken from a performance of the Sugar Hill house band (featuring bassist Doug Wimbish) covering "Cavern", a single by New York City band Liquid Liquid. When originally released on Sugar Hill Records, the record was credited to Grandmaster

& Melle Mel (some international issues carried the credit Grandmaster Flash & Melle Mel). This was done to mislead the general public into believing that Grandmaster Flash participated on the record when in fact he played no part and had already left the Sugar Hill Records label the previous year.

"White Lines" peaked at No. 47 on the Billboard Hot Black Singles chart in 1983. The song fared better in the United Kingdom, reaching number 7 on the UK Singles Chart in July 1984, spending 17 consecutive weeks in the top 40. It was the 13th best-selling single of 1984 in the UK, selling more than several number one hits that year. The song was co-written by Melle Mel and Sylvia Robinson. Originally, it was intended to be an ironic celebration of a cocaine-fueled party lifestyle, but it was abridged with the *"don't do it"* message as a concession to commercial considerations.

The lines: *"A businessman is caught with 24 kilos / He's out on bail and out of jail and that's the way it goes"* refers to car manufacturer - John DeLorean, who in 1982 became entrapped in a scheme to save his company from bankruptcy using drug money. Some of the lyrics in "White Lines" ("something of a phenomenon") echoed lyrics from the song "Cavern" by Liquid Liquid ("slipping in and out of phenomenon") from which the famous bassline was borrowed. As discussed in a 2011 article in the Village Voice, the entire "White Lines" was a note-by-note appropriation of "Cavern", with a rapping track overlaid.

1984

Russell Simmons and Rick Rubin launches Def Jam Records

Def Jam Recordings is an American record label focused predominantly on hip hop and urban music, owned by Universal Music Group. In the UK, the label takes on the name Def Jam UK and is operated through Virgin EMI Records, while in Japan, it is known as Def Jam Japan, operating through Universal Music Japan. Def Jam was co-founded by Rick Rubin in his dormitory in Weinstein Hall at New York University. Def Jam's first release was a single by Rubin's punk-rock group Hose. Russell Simmons joined Rubin shortly after they were introduced to each other, according to one story, by Vincent Gallo. Another cites DJ Jazzy Jay as their connector. Rubin has said he met Simmons on the TV show, Graffiti Rock and recognized him then as "the face of hip hop": "He was five years older than me, and he was already established in the music business. And I had no experience whatsoever." The first single released with the Def Jam Recordings logo was T La Rock & Jazzy Jay's "It's Yours." The first releases with Def Jam Recordings catalog numbers were LL Cool J's "I Need a Beat" and the Beastie Boys' "Rock Hard," both in 1984. The singles sold well, eventually leading to a distribution deal with CBS Records through Columbia Records the following year.

This created a short-lived subsidiary label called OBR Records, short for Original Black Recordings, which catered toward R&B artists—the first artist signed to that imprint was Oran "Juice" Jones, who enjoyed success with his hit single "The Rain", a song about the falling rain outside his window that made him depressed. A few years later, Russell Simmons and Lyor Cohen started an umbrella label called Rush Associated Labels to handle Def Jam and its numerous spinoff labels. RAL became the home to Nice & Smooth and EPMD after both acts were acquired due to the folding of their former label Sleeping Bag Records. Other acts under the RAL umbrella included Redman, Onyx, Flatlinerz, Domino, Warren G and Jayo Felony. Def Jam also signed its first and only thrash metal band, Slayer, in 1986, and the band's third and fourth albums were the only two Def Jam releases to be distributed through Geffen Records under Warner Bros. Records as opposed to

Columbia/CBS. As the decade drew to a close, the label signed Public Enemy, whose controversial lyrical content garnered the company both critical acclaim and disdain. Lyor Cohen became president of Def Jam/RAL in 1988, after winning a power struggle with Rubin, who would shortly thereafter leave the company to form Def American Recordings. Rubin would take Slayer with him to Def American in its initial stages.

Battle rap assumes the spotlight in hip-hop

In 1984, the hip-hop trio U.T.F.O., produced by the R&B group Full Force, released a single titled "Hanging Out," which did not do well. However, it was the single's B side, "Roxanne, Roxanne", a song about a woman who would not respond to their advances, that gained much attention and airplay. Soon afterwards, 14-year-old Lolita Shanté Gooden was walking outside a New York City housing project called Queensbridge, when she heard Tyrone Williams, disc jockey Mr. Magic, and record producer Marley Marl talking about how U.T.F.O. had canceled their appearance at a show they were promoting. Gooden offered to make a hip-hop record that would get back at U.T.F.O., with her taking on the moniker Roxanne Shanté, after her middle name. The three took her up on the idea, with Marley producing "Roxanne's Revenge."

The single was released in late 1984, taking the original beats from an instrumental version of "Roxanne, Roxanne." It was very confrontational and laced with profanities, but was an instant hit that sold over 250,000 copies in the New York area alone. Legal action followed, and it was re-released in early 1985 with new beats and the obscenities removed. Following this, U.T.F.O. and Full Force decided to release their own answer record. While not directly aimed at Roxanne Shanté, this record featured Elease Jack, who took on the moniker of the Real Roxanne (and was soon replaced by Adelaida Martinez). This also was a hit, but it may have also produced an undesired result: while there had been answer records before (such as the semi-disco song "Somebody Else's Guy" and "Games People Play"/"Games Females Play"), they usually ended with the second recording. But in this saga, with a third record in airplay, a whole new trend began. The airwaves were so occupied with the three "Roxanne" records that other MCs decided to get into the act. Over the next year, anywhere from 30 to over 100 answer records (according to different claims) were produced, portraying Roxanne's family, or making various claims about her.

Michael Jackson Moonwalked On TV For The First Time

Michael Jackson took the stage and made an indelible impact on pop culture with his solo performance on

"Motown 25: Yesterday, Today, Forever," a televised celebration of the famous label's creation. The May 16, 1983 broadcast was produced and directed by Don Mischer, who has helped orchestrate other historic moments over the years, including the opening ceremony for the 1996 Olympic Games, where Muhammad Ali made a surprise appearance; Prince's iconic 2007 "Purple Rain" Super Bowl halftime show; and many Oscar ceremonies (not, thankfully for him, 2017's Envelopegate).

Since Motown 25 was intended to showcase the label's greatest hits, Mischer and executive producer Suzanne de Passe initially banned every artist (from Marvin Gaye to the Temptations to Diana Ross) from performing new material. Jackson pushed back, wanting to perform a solo song called "Billie Jean." Mischer recalls the tense moment: "Look, if we let Michael do a new song, who's going to take the phone call from Marvin Gaye on Monday saying, 'Why did you let Michael do a new song and I couldn't do a new song?'"

Mischer and de Passe ended up letting Jackson perform "Billie Jean," with Mischer volunteering to take the call from a presumably ticked-off Marvin Gaye on Monday. For those not alive in 1983 or who may misremember the performance, Jackson's actual moonwalk was surprisingly brief: It lasted only two and a half seconds. There are a few yelps of approval from the fans in the audience, but that moment in itself didn't bring down the house. Like most myths, it has evolved exponentially over the years.

Treacherous Three releases their debut album

The Treacherous Three is the first studio album by American hip hop group Treacherous Three. It was released in 1984 via Sugar Hill Records with distribution of MCA Records and produced by Sylvia Robinson. Complex (magazine) puts the album at number 37 on their 50 Greatest Rap Albums 1980s. The songs "At the Party", "Feel the Heartbeat" and "The Body Rock" were recorded and released from 1980 to 1981 as 12" singles for Bobby Robinson's Enjoy Records and were also compiled on Whip It (1983). The songs "Turning You On", "U.F.O." and "Get Up" were recorded and released in 1983 on Sylvia Robinson's Sugar Hill Records.

TRACKS

"Get Up"

"Turning You On"

"U.F.O."

"The Body Rock"

"Feel the Heartbeat"

"At the Party"

Fat Boys release their First Studio Album

Fat Boys is the self-titled first studio album by hip hop group The Fat Boys on May 29, 1984 by Sutra Records. Album was produced by rap legend Kurtis Blow. LP is dedicated to the memory of Rebecca Wimbely and William (Divine) Santos. Album picked at number 48 on the US Billboard 200, and number 6 on the Top R&B/Hip Hop Albums chart. The album was certified Gold by the RIAA on May 6, 1985. The album features two the Billboard singles: "Jail House Rap" and "Can You Feel It?". The songs "Don't You Dog Me" and "Fat Boys" were performed in the movie Krush Groove during the Disco Fever scene. "Jail House Rap" and "Fat Boys" were performed in the episode of the Soul Train, aired on January 5, 1985.

On November 23, 2012, the album was reissued in a limited-edition CD and vinyl package. The album is housed in a pizza box, with the album itself being a picture disc of pizza, with a special book and bonus material (downloadable for the vinyl version). XXL revisiting the Fat Boys' iconic debut album 30 years later. Buff a.k.a. The Human Beat Box (Darren Robinson), Prince Markie Dee (Mark Morales) and Kool Rock-Ski (Damon Wimbley) were hip-hop's first brand, jumping out of helicopters in Swatch commercials and demolishing buffets in movies. Their manager is a Swiss-born promoter named Charlie Stettler, the owner of his label-management company Tin Pan Apple. In 1983, he put on a hip-hop talent contest at

Radio City Music Hall, and the Fat Boys-then rapping as Disco 3-were the unexpected walk-on champs.

"Stick 'Em" was the song they used to win the contest. Stettler took the group to his native Switzerland. And though they arrived in Europe as the Disco 3, the group flew back to New York as the Fat Boys. Charlie Stettler hooked up the group with producer Kurtis Blow who gave them their signature sound. Kurtis Blow enlisted Run-DMC drum-machine programmer Larry Smith and bassist Davy "DMX" Reeves, both of whom were behind some of the best records of the era to work on it. "Stick 'Em" was the first thing that they recorded with Kurtis Blow. Charlie Stettler also got Swatch to sponsor 1984's Fresh Festival Tour and convinced Russell Simmons to add the Fat Boys to a line-up that included Run-DMC, Whodini and Newcleus. The Fat Boys released 3 singles from this album: "Jail House Rap", "Can You Feel It?" and "Fat Boys". The group released 5 official music videos on the songs from this album: "Fat Boys", "Jail House Rap", "Can You Feel It?", "Stick 'Em" and "Don't You Dog Me".

TRACKS

Side A:

"Jail House Rap"

"Stick 'Em"

"Can You Feel It?"

Side B:

"Fat Boys"

"The Place to Be"

"Human Beat Box"

"Don't You Dog Me"

2012 bonus tracks:

"Reality"

"International Love"

"All You Can Eat"

"Fat Boys Promo (Rap Attack)"

"Fat Boys And Charlie Stettler Interview (Mr. Magic's Rap Attack - 4/20/84)"

"Fat Boys Interview A (Mr. Magic's Rap Attack - 1/23/84)"

"Fat Boys Interview B (Mr. Magic's Rap Attack - 1/23/84)"

"Mr. Magic announcing The Disco 3 as winners at Radio City Music Hall on May 23, 1983" (hidden bonus track)

GREG BROUSSARD RELEASES HIS DEBUT

'On the Nile' is the debut studio album by American hip hop artist Greg Broussard under the alias of The Egyptian Lover. The album belongs to the electro hop genre, and involves party themed music involving Broussard attracted women and escapism. The album was released in 1984, by Egyptian Empire Records. It charted on Billboard's Pop Albums chart. Prior to recording On the Nile, Broussard recorded some music for the film Breaking & Entering. Broussard found that he had so much fun in the studio recording it, he wanted to return to do a solo project. This led to the beginning of recording the song "Egypt, Egypt". The initial song was going to be called "Beast Beats". After his sister disapproved of the themes of "Beast Beats", he changed the beat and looked into his rhyme book and created the song "Egypt, Egypt". Broussard explained that he developed the music on the album as he would do a DJ show, finding he "wasn't a good composer or producer or anything like that. I just made the record as I would DJ, "I'm going to cut this record in, now I'm going to cut this record in." So it had no arrangement on the record. Everything was cutting like a DJ and that was kind of rare back in the day because nobody did records like that. So this one had no verse-chorus breakdown, this is just all over the place, and it was a good party record because this is how DJs cut the records back then, so that's what I did."

"Egypt, Egypt" was written as something Broussard could play to "something I could play at dances to let people know my name". Broussard opined that the song "was actually a riff from "Planet Rock." I just played it half-speed. Instead of doing the whole "Planet Rock" thing, I played it half-speed and came up with that." When discussing his song "My House (On the Nile)", Broussard expressed that he grew up in Los Angeles "not having much of anything" and songs such as "My House (On the Nile)" "was a fantasy to escape from reality and I expressed that way of life in my songs." Broussard expanded on the themes of escape, stating that when he was "growing up in the hood, the first thing you want to do is get out the hood. So in my mind I took myself out the hood and I just took myself to any place I could find, which was probably just Egypt at the time."

As part of electro hop genre, Broussard's music drew from musicians such as Parliament/Funkadelic, Prince and Afrika Bambaataa. Broussard uses electronic instruments and voice manipulators in his music, specifically noting that he often applies "that robot voice and that electronic music—using real electronic sounds from spaceships from outer space. To me, it was the best way to escape from where I grew up"

TRACKS

Side A:

"My House (On the Nile)"

What Is a D.J. If He Can't Scratch"

"Girls"

"Computer Love (Sweet Dreams)"

Side B:

"Egypt, Egypt"

"I Cry (Night After Night)"

"Unreal"

"And My Beat Goes Boom"

Whodini releases Second Album

'Escape' is the second studio album by the hip-hop group Whodini. The album was recorded at Battery Studios in London, where the group worked with producer Larry Smith after their management could not find them a producer. Whodini member Jalil Hutchins convinced Smith, his friend, to produce the album when Smith needed money after a friend's hospitalisation. Although the group originally intended to record more rock-oriented material for the album, its music has a predominantly synthesizer-based backing, with a rhythm and blues influence. The album was a critical success upon release, and was praised by NME and Robert Christgau. It was also commercially successful, being the first hip-hop album to chart within the U.S. top 40, and was also one of the first to be certified platinum by the RIAA.

After working on their debut self-titled album, Whodini embarked on a three-month European tour. Two-and-a-half weeks into this tour, they were joined by Kangol Kid and UTFO. The group had also planned to tour in Israel and Australia following their European tour, but refused to do so, as they had been away from home for three weeks and found the tour "rigorous". Singer-songwriter Jalil Hutchins later said, "Somebody should've stepped in and made us [continue the tour]." Whodini member John Fletcher (Ecstasy) said that the group thought European audiences would be unfamiliar with their music, but they "found that lots of kids, lots of club owners, had made a real effort to get hold of our music. When we discovered that, we realized that the music we were working with really was universal, that we didn't have to think of a particular market. People everywhere like to dance, sweat and party, and they like the same kind of sounds."

The group worked well with German producer Conny Plank on Whodini, and were trying to find a similar producer. According to Hutchins, "Conny had an understanding of what hip hop was, and if we had an understanding of how to explain it to these musicians who were far ahead of us, we would've produced some special records. On the next album, we decided that we needed to get somebody from [the US] that understood where we were coming from." Although Jive Records initially hired

Russell Simmons and Larry Smith to produce Escape, commitments in New York kept Simmons from recording sessions. Hutchins had met Smith at Disco Fever in New York City; although they were friends and often discussed music, he said that they did not originally consider working together. Jive Records could not find a producer, and Hutchins asked Smith to come to Europe and produce the album. The producer initially refused for financial reasons, but called Hutchins the following day saying that he needed money to pay a hospital bill for a friend who had his finger tips ripped off. Smith and Hutchins then quickly met to develop music to show to the label, recording the bass for "Five Minutes of Funk".

The music on 'Escape', in particular "Five Minutes of Funk", was originally intended to be rock music oriented, with Hutchins suggesting that the song would be similar to the "rawer" work of groups such as The Isley Brothers. Whodini had planned to use a Minimoog synthesizer on the track, although Smith left his at home, assuming that he could find one in the United Kingdom. Unable to locate one, the group then heard Run–DMC's "Rock Box" and decided to follow a more R&B-oriented direction. Smith said that although he was told by Jive Records to make the album sound like Run–DMC, he "didn't want to do exactly that. Whodini's a bit more adult, I think, and rap's not just for kids anymore."

The record has been called "rhythm & blues-based rap", and has been cited as a major influence on new jack swing

—a hip-hop-influenced form of funk which became the dominant form of contemporary R&B from 1987 to 1993. Nelson George described Escape's music as a style which "black radio embraces", specifically a "radio-friendly, singles-oriented hip hop", as opposed to the "hard-core, more rhyme-centered rap". Retrospective commentary on their music suggested that, although the group sounded tame when compared to the later work of artists such as Too Short and Ol' Dirty Bastard, as well as groups like 2 Live Crew, Whodini were considered "raunchy and racy" during the mid-1980s on songs such as "Freaks Come Out at Night".

Unlike other hip-hop musicians, Whodini's backing music and beats were synthesizer-based. Escape contains tracks with minimal musical backing, such as "Big Mouth" and "Friends", and faster-paced music such as "Escape (I Need a Break)"..Hutchins believed that the Fender Jazz Bass was part of Whodini's signature sound, and used it on "Five Minutes of Funk". Escape's lyrics are generally egocentric, but also explored the difficulty of city life ("Escape (I Need a Break)"), failed romance ("Friends") and New York's party lifestyle ("Freaks Come Out at Night").

TRACKS

Side A:

"Five Minutes of Funk"

"Freaks Come out at Night"

"Featuring Grand Master Dee"

"Big Mouth"

Side B:

"Escape (I Need a Break)"

"Friends"

"Out of Control"

"We Are Whodini"

Run–DMC Debut Album Release

Run–DMC is the debut studio album of American hip hop group Run–DMC. Produced in 1984, it was considered groundbreaking for its time, presenting a harder, more aggressive form of hip hop. The album's sparse beats and aggressive rhymes were in sharp contrast with the light, funky sound that was popular in hip hop at the time. With the album, the group has been regarded by music writers as pioneering the movement of new school hip hop of the mid-1980s. The album was reissued as a "Deluxe Edition" in 2005 with four bonus tracks.

The album has been regarded by music writers as one of

early hip hop's best albums and a landmark release of the new school hip hop movement in the 1980s. According to journalist Peter Shapiro, the album's 1983 double-single release "It's Like That"/"Sucker MCs" "completely changed hip-hop ... rendering everything that preceded it distinctly old school with one fell swoop." Run–DMC rapped over the most sparse of musical backing tracks in hip hop at the time: a drum machine and a few scratches, with rhymes that harangued weak rappers and contrasted them to the group's success. "It's Like That" is an aggressively delivered message rap whose social commentary has been defined variously as "objective fatalism", "frustrated and renunciatory", and just plain "reportage".

TRACKS

Side A:

"Hard Times"

"Rock Box"

"Jam-Master Jay"

"Scratchin'" by Magic Disco Machine

"Hollis Crew (Krush-Groove 2)"

"Sucker M.C.'s (Krush-Groove 1)"

"Live at the Disco Fever"

. . .

Side B:

"It's Like That"

"Wake Up"

"30 Days"

"Jay's Game"

1985

Sugarhill Records goes into Bankruptcy

The Sugar Hill label's first record was "Rapper's Delight (1979) by The Sugarhill Gang, which was also the first Top 40 hip-hop single. Afterwards The Sequence, Grandmaster Flash and The Furious Five, Funky Four Plus One, Crash Crew, Treacherous Three, and the West Street Mob, joined the label. Sugar Hill's in-house producer and arranger was Clifton "Jiggs" Chase. The in-house recording engineer was Steve Jerome. Joe and Sylvia's sons Joey and Leland were also active in the business.

In the early 1980s, the Robinsons bought Levy out. They enjoyed several years of success. Sylvia produced several music videos and a young Spike Lee making his first music video for the song "White Lines" (performed by Melle Mel and The Furious Five). Joe Robinson was innovative in the business end. He was the first to introduce a cassette single. He also worked with TVS Television Network executive Tom Ficara to produce the Fresh Groove TV series to feature these music videos when MTV would not run them. The success of Fresh Groove forced MTV to establish Yo! MTV Raps, and rap music videos were now on a mainstream cable network. A controversial distribution deal with MCA Records ended up in protracted litigation, and, finally, the label closed down in 1986.

Run–DMC's Second Album Release

King of Rock is the second studio album by American hip-hop group Run–DMC. Produced in 1985, the album saw the group adopting a more rock-influenced sound, with several tracks prominently featuring heavy guitar riffs.

TRACKS

"Rock the House"

"King of Rock"

"You Talk Too Much"

"Jam-Master Jammin'"

"Roots, Rap, Reggae" (feat. Yellowman)

"Can You Rock It Like This"

"You're Blind"

"It's Not Funny"

"Darryl and Joe (Krush-Groove 3)"

Deluxe edition bonus tracks:

"Slow and Low (Demo)"

"Together Forever (Krush-Groove 4) (Live)"

"Jam-Master Jammin' (Remix, Long Version)"

"King of Rock (Live, from Live Aid)"

Too Short's second album

'Players' is the second studio album by American Oakland-based rapper Too Short. It was released in 1985 via 75 Girls Records. Audio production of the entire record was handled by Dean Hodges, who also served as executive producer.

TRACKS

"Players"

"From Here To New York"

"Don't Ever Stop"

"Wild, Wild West"

"Everytime"

"Dance (Don't Geek)"

"Coke Dealers"

LL Cool J releases debut album

'Radio' is the debut album by rapper, LL Cool J. It was released on November 18, 1985, by Def Jam Recordings and Columbia Records. It was also Def Jam's first full-length album release. The album was recorded during 1984 and 1985 in sessions at Chung King House of Metal in New York City and was produced primarily by Rick Rubin, who provided a sparse, minimal production style. The album also features a sound punctuated by DJ scratching, often brief samples, and emphasis of the downbeat. LL Cool J's aggressive b-boy lyrics explored themes of inner city culture, teenage promiscuity, and braggadocio raps.

A significant sales success for a hip hop record at the time, Radio became a Billboard chart hit and sold over 500,000 copies within its first five months of release. By 1989, it had been certified platinum by the Recording Industry Association of America for sales surpassing one million copies in the United States. Initial reception of the album was generally positive, with praise given to LL Cool J's lyricism and Rubin's production. It has since been recognized by critics as LL Cool J's best album.

Radio belonged to a pivotal moment in hip hop's culture and history, reflecting the new school and ghetto-blaster subculture in the United States during the mid-1980s. The album's success contributed to the displacement of the old school with the new school form and to the genre's mainstream success during this period. It was also a career breakthrough for LL Cool J and Rick Rubin. 'Radio' has been recognized by music journalists as one of the first artistically cohesive and commercially successful hip hop albums.

It all started on March 1984, when NYU student Rick Rubin and promoter-manager Russell Simmons founded the then-independent Def Jam label. Sixteen- year–old St. Albans, Queens native, James Todd Smith was making demos in his grandparents' home. His grandfather, a jazz saxophonist, purchased him $ 2,000 worth of stereo equipment, including two turntables, an audio mixer and an amplifier. Smith later discussed his childhood background and rapping, saying that "By the time I got that equipment, I was already a rapper. In this neighborhood, the kids grow up in rap. It's like speaking Spanish if you grow up in an all-Spanish house. I got into it when I was about 9, and since then all I wanted was to make a record and hear it on the radio." By using the mixing table he had received from his grandfather, Smith produced and mixed his own demos and sent them to various record companies throughout New York City, including Simmons' and Rubin's Def Jam Recordings.

Under his new stage name, LL Cool J (an acronym for Ladies Love Cool James), Smith was signed by Def Jam, which led to the release of his first official record, the 12-inch single "I Need a Beat" (1984). The single was a hard-hitting, streetwise b-boy song with spare beats and ballistic rhymes. Smith later discussed his search for a label, stating "I sent my demo to many different companies, but it was Def Jam where I found my home." That same year, Smith made his professional debut concert performance at Manhattan Center High School. In a later interview, LL Cool J recalled the experience, stating "They pushed the lunch room tables together and me and my DJ, Cut Creator, started playing. ... As soon as it was over there were girls screaming and asking for autographs. Right then and there I said 'This is what I want to do'." LL's debut single sold over 100,000 copies and helped establish both Def Jam as a label and Smith as a rapper. The commercial success of "I Need a Beat", along with the Beastie Boys' single "Rock Hard" (1984), helped lead Def Jam to a distribution deal with Columbia Records the following year.

LL Cool J dropped out of Andrew Jackson High School in Queens to record his first studio album, also the first LP to be issued by Def Jam. Recording sessions for the album took place at Chung King Studios in Manhattan's Chinatown under Rubin's direction throughout 1984 and 1985. Notable from the personnel line-up was LL's DJ Jay Philpot, better known as "Cut Creator". A Queens native and former trombonist, Philpot met LL at a block party and they began performing together. The audio mastering was handled by engineer Herb Powers at 130 West 42nd Street in the Frankford Wayne Mastering Labs and the album was set for release as Radio in November 1985, containing a dedication in the liner notes from LL Cool J to his mother and his grandparents. The album's release had been anticipated by many rap fans following LL Cool J's appearance in the hip hop movie Krush Groove, which was based on the beginnings of the Def Jam label and featured the single "I Can't Live Without My Radio" from Radio.

TRACKS

Side A:

"I Can't Live Without My Radio"

"You Can't Dance"

"Dear Yvette"

"I Can Give You More"

"Dangerous"

"El Shabazz"

Side B:

"Rock the Bells"

"I Need a Beat (Remix)"

"That's a Lie" (featuring Russell Rush)

"You'll Rock"

"I Want You"

The Fat Boys releases Second Album

The Fat Boys Are Back is the second studio album by hip hop group The Fat Boys, released on June 1, 1985 by Sutra Records. Album was produced by rap legend Kurtis Blow. Album picked at number 63 on the US Billboard 200, and number 11 on the Top R&B/Hip Hop Albums chart. The album was certified Gold by the RIAA on January 9, 1986. The album features three the Billboard singles: "The Fat Boys Are Back", "Hard Core Reggae" and "Don't Be Stupid". The song "Pump It Up" was performed in the movie Krush Groove during the Disco Fever scene.

TRACKS

"The Fat Boys Are Back"

"Don't Be Stupid"

"Human Beat Box"

"Yes, Yes, Y'All"

"Hard Core Reggae"

"Pump It Up"

"Fat Boys Scratch"

"Rock 'N' Roll"

Mantronix releases their debut album

TRACKS

"Bassline"

"Needle to the Groove"

"Mega-Mix"

"Hardcore Hip-Hop"

"Ladies"

"Get Stupid "Fresh" Part I"

"Fresh Is the Word"

BONUS TRACKS

In February 2006, Virgin/EMI re-released the album in the UK with five bonus tracks and new cover art:

"Ladies (Revived)"

"Bassline (Stretched)"

"Hardcore Hip Hop (NME Mix)"

"Ladies (Dub)"

"Ladies (Instrumental)"

First extended play by Los Angeles-based electro-hop group

World Class is the first extended play by Los Angeles-based electro-hop group "World Class Wreckin' Cru." It was released in 1985 under the Kru-Cut record label. Songs on the album included "Juice" and "Surgery", which were popular singles on the underground West Coast scene. The album cover was used as a form of ridicule to Dr. Dre in Eazy-E's diss song "Real Muthaphuckkin G's" showing the album images of Dr. Dre on the album wearing flashy clothing and makeup. The style was later attributed to the fashion sense of Prince which was heavily popular at the time. It was also parodied by Luther Campbell on the song "Cowards Of Compton".

TRACKS

"Planet"

"World Class"

"Surgery" (Remix)

"Juice" (Edited version)

"(Horney) Computer"

"Gang Bang You're Dead"

"Lovers" (featuring Mona Lisa Young)

Schoolly D's debut

'Schoolly D' is the self-titled debut album which was originally released on Schoolly D records in 1985 and in 1990 on Jive Records, and was produced by Schoolly D and DJ Code Money. The album featured three singles, "Put Your Filas On." "P.S.K. What Does It Mean?" and "Gucci Time." Schoolly D is from West Philly and known as hip-hop's first gangsta rapper.

ERIC REESE

TRACKS

"I Don't Like Rock & Roll"

"Put Your Filas On"

"Free Style Rapping"

"P.S.K. What Does It Mean?"

"Gucci Time"

"Free Style Cutting"

1986

WHODINI'S THIRD ALBUM

'Back in Black' was recorded in London and released via Jive Records in 1986. Like on the group's previous work, audio production was handled by Larry Smith. The album peaked at #35 on the Billboard 200, #4 on the Top R&B/Hip-Hop Albums, and was certified gold by Recording Industry Association of America on June 23, 1986.

TRACKS

"Funky Beat"

"One Love"

"Growing Up"

ERIC REESE

"I'm A Ho"

"How Dare You"

"Fugitive"

"Echo Scratch"

"Last Night (I Had A Long Talk With Myself)"

"The Good Part"

The Fat Boys releases third studio album

'Big & Beautiful' is the third studio album by hip hop group - The Fat Boys, released in May 1986 through Sutra Records. This was their last release on this label.

TRACKS

"Sex Machine"

"Go For It"

"Breakdown"

"Double-O Fat Boys"

"Big & Beautiful"

"Rapp Symphony (In C-Minor)"

"Human Beat Box, Part III"

"In The House"

"Beat Box Is Rockin'"

Run-DMC's Third Album Release

'Raising Hell' is the third album by Run-DMC. The breakthrough album trumped standing perceptions of commercial viability for hip-hop groups, achieving triple-platinum status and receiving critical attention from quarters that had previously ignored hip hop, dismissing it as a fad. Raising Hell features the well-known cover "Walk This Way" featuring Steven Tyler and Joe Perry of Aerosmith. While the song was not the group's first fusion of rock and hip hop (the group's earlier singles "Rock Box" and "King of Rock" were), it was the first such fusion significantly impacting the charts, becoming the first rap song to crack the top 5 of The Billboard Hot 100. Raising Hell peaked at No. 1 on Billboard's Top R&B Albums chart as the first hip hop/rap album to do so, and at No. 6 on the Billboard 200.

Raising Hell was voted the fifth best album of 1986 in the Pazz & Jop, an annual poll of American critics nationwide, published by The Village Voice. It ranked number 8 among the "Albums of the Year" by NME. Robert Christgau, the poll's creator, wrote in a contemporary review, "Without benefit of a 'Rock Box' or 'King of Rock,' this is [Run–DMC's] most uncompromising and compelling album, all hard beats and declaiming voices." Richard Cromelin was less enthusiastic in his review for the Los Angeles Times, writing that the group's style sounded somewhat repetitive and limited: "If the same old boasts are wearing thin and the misogyny gets grating, the beats are infectious and varied and the vocal trade-offs can be dazzling."

TRACKS

"Peter Piper"

"It's Tricky"

"My Adidas"

"Walk This Way"

"Is It Live"

"Perfection"

"Hit It Run"

"Raising Hell"

"You Be Illin'"

"Dumb Girl"

"Son of Byford"

"Proud to Be Black"

DELUXE EDITION BONUS TRACKS

"My Adidas" (a cappella)

"Walk This Way" (demo)

"Lord of Lyrics" (demo)

"Raising Hell Radio Tour Spot"

"Live at the Apollo Raw Vocal Commercial"

2 Live Crew releases First Album

The '2 Live Crew Is What We Are' is the debut album by the 2 Live Crew. It was released in 1986 on Luke Records to a great deal of controversy and promptly was certified gold by the RIAA. It includes the hits "We Want Some Pussy", "Throw the 'D'", and "Cuttin' It Up". Bob Rosenberg, a south Florida DJ who would later form the dance-pop group - Will to Power, remixed and edited the song "Beat Box". In Florida, it was deemed obscene, and one store clerk was charged with felony "corruption of a minor" for selling it to a 14-year-old girl. The clerk was later acquitted.

TRACKS

"2 Live Is What We Are..."

"We Want Some Pussy"

"Check It Out Yall"

"Get It Girl"

"Throw The 'D'"

"Cut It Up"

"Beat Box" (Remix)

"Mr. Mixx On The Mix!!"

Too Short drops a third album

Raw, Uncut and X-Rated is the third studio album by American Oakland-based rapper Too Short. It was recorded and released in November 5, 1986 via 75 Girls Records.

TRACKS

"Invasion Of Flat Booty Bitches"

"She's A Bitch"

"Oakland, California"

"The Bitch Sucks Dick"

"Short Side/Blow Job Betty"

Beastie Boys releases First Album

'Licensed to Ill' was released on November 15, 1986 by Def Jam and Columbia Records, and became the first rap LP to top the Billboard album chart. It is one of Columbia Records' fastest-selling debut records to date and was certified Diamond by the Recording Industry Association of America in 2015 for shipping over ten million copies in the United States. The group originally wanted to title the album Don't Be a Faggot, but Columbia Records refused to release the album under this title—arguing that it was homophobic—and pressured Russell Simmons, the Beastie Boys' manager and head of Def Jam Recordings at the time, into forcing them to choose another name. Adam Horovitz has since apologized for the album's earlier title.

Kerry King of Slayer made an appearance on the album playing lead guitar on "No Sleep Till Brooklyn" and appeared in the music video which is a parody of glam metal. The name of the song itself is a spoof on Motörhead's No Sleep 'til Hammersmith album. King's appearance on the track came about because Rick Rubin was producing both bands simultaneously (Slayer's Reign in Blood was originally released a month earlier on Def Jam). CBS/Fox Video released a video album of the five Licensed to Ill videos, plus "She's on It" in 1987 to capitalize on the album's success. A laserdisc version was also released in Japan. All versions of the CBS/Fox release are currently out of print because the rights to the album passed from

Columbia and Sony Music to Universal Music Group, and also because of the acrimonious nature of the band's departure from Def Jam Records. Until the 2005 release of the CD/DVD Solid Gold Hits, none of the Def Jam-era videos had been included on any subsequent Beastie Boys video compilations. The Solid Gold Hits DVD includes the videos for "Fight for Your Right" and "No Sleep Till Brooklyn", as well as a live version of "Brass Monkey" from a 2004 concert.

TRACKS

"Rhymin & Stealin"

"The New Style"

"She's Crafty"

"Posse in Effect"

"Slow Ride"

"Girls"

"Fight for Your Right"

"No Sleep till Brooklyn"

"Paul Revere"

"Hold It Now, Hit It"

"Brass Monkey"

"Slow and Low"

"Time to Get Ill"

Afrika Bambaataa releases "Planet Rock"

Planet Rock: The Album by Afrika Bambaataa & Soulsonic Force, was released in 1986 as a collection of previous singles. The song "Planet Rock" was one of the earliest hits of the hip hop music genre and remains one of its pioneering recordings. The single's liner notes include members of Kraftwerk with the songwriting credits. In creating the track, portions of Kraftwerk's "Numbers" and "Trans-Europe Express" were interpolated (re-recorded in the studio, rather than through the use of a digital sampler), along with portions of songs by Captain Sky and Ennio Morricone.

TRACKS

"Planet Rock"

"Looking for the Perfect Beat"

"Renegades of Funk"

"Frantic Situation"

"Who You Funkin' With?"

"Go-Go Pop"

ERIC REESE

"They Made a Mistake"

Personnel

Arthur Baker – producer, mixing

Keith LeBlanc – producer

Herb Powers Jr. – mastering

Latin Rascals – remixing

Afrika Bambaataa – producer, mixing

John Aquilino – illustrations, hand lettering

Jay Burnett – mixing

Albert Cabrera – remixing

Skip McDonald – producer

Tony Moran – remixing

John Robie – producer, mixing

LeRoi Evans – producer, mixing

Rae Serrano – producer

Adrian Sherwood – mixing

Andy Wallace – mixing

Doug Wimbish – producer

Monica Lynch – art direction

Steven Miglio – artwork, design

Fats Comet – producer, mixing

M.C. G.L.O.B.E. – additional vocals

Salt-n-Pepa Album Debut

Hot, Cool, & Vicious is the debut album by Salt-n-Pepa. Released by Next Plateau Records on December 8, 1986, it was one of the first albums to be released by an all-female rap group. Hot, Cool, & Vicious also became the first album by a female rap group act to attain gold and platinum status in America. The album features the songs "The Show Stoppa (Is Stupid Fresh)" and "I'll Take Your Man", recorded and released prior to the full album's release. It also includes R&B radio favorites "Tramp" and "My Mic Sound Nice", but it was after the 1987 addition of the dance-rap single "Push It" (US #19, UK #2), along with the replacement of two other tracks with remixed versions, that the album was propelled to gold status, then platinum status in America. The single itself was also certified platinum. In 1998, Hot, Cool, & Vicious was listed in The Source's 100 Best Rap Albums.

TRACKS

"Push It" (Remix)

"Beauty and the Beat"

"Tramp"

"I'll Take Your Man"

"It's Alright"

"Chick on the Side"

"I Desire"

"The Show Stoppa"

"My Mic Sound Nice"

EGYPTIAN LOVER'S SECOND ALBUM RELEASE

One Track Mind was released in 1986 for Egyptian Empire Records and was produced by Egyptian Lover himself. The album reached #37 on the Billboard R&B albums chart and produced two charting singles, "The Lover" and "Freak-a-Holic".

TRACKS

"One Track Mind"

"You're So Fine"

"The Dark Side of Egypt"

"Livin' on the Nile"

"Freak-A-Holic"

"The Lover"

"The Alezby Inn"

"Los Angeles"

"Kinky Nation (Kingdom Kum)"

Just-Ice's first album

'Back to the Old School' is the debut album by American rapper Just-Ice. It was released in 1986, and was produced by Kurtis Mantronik. The album has been described as a classic early hip-hop album and revolutionary for its time by Allmusic.

TRACKS

"Cold Gettin' Dumb"

"Love Story"

"Back to the Old School"

"Latoya"

"Gangster of Hip Hop"

"Little Bad Johnny"

"Put the Record Back On"

"Turbo-Charged"

"Cold Gettin' Dumb II" (Originally a 12-inch single, it was added when the album was released on CD)

"That Girl is a Slut" (Originally a b-side, it was added when the album was released on CD)

Debut Album from Legend "Kool Moe Dee"

Kool Moe Dee is the eponymous debut solo studio album by American rapper Kool Moe Dee from the Treacherous Three. It was released in 1986 via Jive Records, and produced by Teddy Riley, Bryan "Chuck" New, LaVaba Mallison, Pete Q. Harris, Robert Wells and Kool Moe Dee. The album peaked at number 83 on the Billboard 200, number 20 on the Top R&B/Hip-Hop Albums and sold over 300,000 copies. The record spawned four singles: "Go See the Doctor", "Rock Steady", "Dumb Dick (Richard)" and "Do You Know What Time It Is?", but only its lead single, "Go See the Doctor" has reached music charts, peaking at #89 on the Billboard Hot 100 and #82 on the UK Singles Chart. "Kool Moe Dee" was released on CD in 1989.

TRACKS

"Go See the Doctor"

"Dumb Dick (Richard)"

"Bad Mutha"

"Little Jon"

"Do You Know What Time it Is?"

"Rock Steady"

"Monster Crack"

"The Best"

"I'm Kool Moe Dee"

"Go See the Doctor" (Uncensored version)

Stetsasonic releases First Album

'On Fire' is the debut album from Stetsasonic. The group is famous for being one of hip hop's first live bands, a style that was influential over a number of later artists such as the Roots. The album was originally released in 1986; record label Tommy Boy Records re-released it in 2001 on compact disc for the first time with three bonus tracks. In 1998, the album was selected as one of The Source's 100 Best Rap Albums.

TRACKS

"4 Ever My Beat"

"My Rhyme"

"Just Say Stet"

"Faye"

"4 Ever My Mouth"

"Rock De La Stet"

"Go Stetsa I"

"On Fire"

"Bust That Groove"

"Paul's Groove"

"4 Ever My Beat [Beat Bongo Mix]"

"Go Stetsa I [Remix]"

"A.F.R.I.C.A. [Norman Cook Remix]"

The Skinny Boys Debut Album Release

'Weightless' was released in 1986 for Warlock Records and was produced by Mark Bush and Chuck Chillout. The lead track, "Jockbox," is used as the opening theme for the Comedy Central series, "Workaholics."

TRACKS

"Jockbox"

"Unity"

"Get Funky"

"Weightless"

"Ill"

"Feed Us The Beat"

"Awesome"

"Rip The Cut"

"Skinny Boys

Doug E. Fresh releases first album

Oh, My God! was released in 1986 on Reality Records, a short-lived subsidiary of the legendary - Fantasy Records, and was produced by Dennis Bell and Ollie Cotton. The album had only moderate success when it was released, peaking at #21 on the Top R&B Albums chart. Today, the album is considered one of the greatest hip-hop albums of all time, but it has never been released on CD. This album has also been known to contain one of the first horror-core songs with "Play This Only at Night," which used an interpolation of the theme music of the movie Phantasm.

TRACKS

"Nuthin'"

"The Show" (Oh, My God! Remix)

"Leave It up to the Cut Professor"

"Lovin' Ev'ry Minute of It" (Cyclone Ride)

"She Was the Type of Girl

"Abortion"- 4:21

"Chill Will Cuttin' it Up"

"Play This Only at Night"

"All the Way to Heaven"

1987

BOOGIE DOWN PRODUCTIONS' DEBUT ALBUM

'Criminal Minded' was released on March 3, 1987 by B-Boy Records. Considered a highly influential hip-hop album, it is also credited with providing a prototype for the East Coast gangsta rap which emerged in the following decades. Since its release, it has been sampled, interpolated and paraphrased. The album's samples and direct influences were unusual at the time, ranging from liberal use of dancehall reggae (as well as the more commonly used James Brown) to rock music artists such as AC/DC, The Beatles and Billy Joel. The album was eventually certified Gold by the RIAA.

Initially, the album sold at least several hundred thousand copies; however, the relationship between the group and B-Boy Records quickly deteriorated when the label, headed by Jack Allen and Bill Kamarra, was allegedly slow to pay royalties. A lawsuit was launched, which was eventually settled out-of-court. Having left B-Boy Records, new friend Ice-T introduced BDP to Warner Bros. Records' Benny Medina, head of the label's Black-music division, who promptly agreed to sign the duo in principle to a new record deal. However, it was rescinded after La Rock's death.

By this time, Sterling had befriended a neighborhood teenager named Derrick "D-Nice" Jones, who did a human beat boxing routine for the group. One evening, Jones was assaulted by some local hoodlums and he later called Sterling to run interference. The next day, Sterling and a group of others came to the stoop where the offending parties lived. Sterling's intention was to try and mediate things, but one of the hoods pulled out a gun and began shooting at random. In the ensuing confusion, Sterling was hit in the neck. Critically wounded, he died an hour later in hospital, leaving behind an infant son.

Public Enemy's Drops their First Album

Yo! Bum Rush the Show is the debut album by American hip hop group Public Enemy. It was recorded at Spectrum City Studios in Hempstead, New York, and released on February 10, 1987, by Def Jam Recordings and Columbia Records. The album became one of the fastest-selling hip hop records, but was controversial among radio stations and critics, in part because of its black nationalist messaging. It has since been regarded as one of the genre's best and most influential albums.

DJ Jazzy Jeff and The Fresh Prince releases
Debut Album

'Rock the House' was released on April 7, 1987, in the United States, and was subsequently re-issued in 1988 in Europe and the United Kingdom. Three tracks from the album were released as singles: "The Magnificent Jazzy Jeff", "A Touch of Jazz" and "Girls Ain't Nothing But Trouble". When the album was released on CD in 1988, the rerecorded version of "Girls Ain't Nothing But Trouble", which was released as a single after 'He's the DJ, I'm the Rapper' ran its course, replaced the original 1986 recording. The original version also never appeared on the duo's greatest-hits album.

TRACKS

Side One:

"Girls Ain't Nothing but Trouble"

"Just One of Those Days"

"Rock the House" (Live, NY Union Square)

"Taking It to the Top"

"The Magnificent Jazzy Jeff"

Side Two:

"Just Rockin'"

"Guys Ain't Nothing but Trouble"

"A Touch of Jazz"

"Don't Even Try It"

"Special Announcement"

Dana Dane's Debut Album

'Dana Dane with Fame' was released in 1987 on Profile Records and was produced by legendary producer, Hurby Luv Bug. Dana Dane with Fame achieved great success, peaking at #46 on the Billboard 200 and #2 on the Top R&B/Hip-Hop Albums. In addition to that, the album also featured four charting singles: "Nightmares," "Cinderfella Dana Dane," "Delancey Street," and "This be the Def Beat," which made it to #21, #11, #44, and #30 on the Hot R&B/Hip-Hop Singles & Tracks.

TRACKS

"Dedication"

"Cinderfella Dana Dane"

"This be the Def Beat"

"Dana Dane with Fame"

"Delancey Street"

"We Wanna Party"

"Nightmares"

"Keep the Groove"

"Love at First Sight"

LL Cool J releases second studio album

Bigger and Deffer (abbreviated as BAD on the album cover) is the second studio album by LL Cool J, released on May 29, 1987 by Def Jam Recordings and Columbia Records. It is remembered most for containing the first commercially successful "rap ballad", "I Need Love". It also contains the single "Go Cut Creator Go", which paid homage to his DJ, and the breakthrough single in the U.K. "I'm Bad". With over two million copies sold in the United States alone, it stands as one of LL Cool J's biggest career albums.

ERIC REESE

TRACKS

"I'm Bad"

"Kanday"

"Get Down"

"The Bristol Hotel"

"My Rhyme Ain't Done"

"Go Cut Creator Go"

"The Breakthrough"

"I Need Love"

"Ahh, Let's Get Ill"

"The Do Wop"

"On the Ill Tip (Skit)"

Eric B. and Rakim's Drops "Paid in Full"

The album, 'Paid in Full' by hip-hop duo Eric B. & Rakim, was released on July 7, 1987, by Island-subsidiary label - 4th & B'way Records. The duo recorded the album at hip hop producer Marley Marl's home studio and Power Play Studios in New York City, following Rakim's response to Eric B.'s search for a rapper to complement his disc jockey work in 1985. The album peaked at number fifty-eight on the Billboard 200 chart and produced five singles: "Eric B. Is President", "I Ain't No Joke", "I Know You Got Soul", "Move the Crowd", and "Paid in Full".

Ice-T's First Album Release

'Rhyme Pays' is the first album released by West-Coast rapper, Ice-T. It was released on July 28, 1987 by Sire Records. The album peaked at number 93 on the US Billboard 200 and number 23 on the Top R&B/Hip-Hop Albums charts, and was certified gold by the Recording Industry Association of America (RIAA).

MC Shan releases debut album

Down by Law is the debut album by East Coast hip-hop artist MC Shan. Released at the height of the Bridge Wars, a feud between artists started by South Bronx's KRS-One responding to the Queensbridge anthem "The Bridge". The song's swearing was edited out of the album. The album contains the diss track, "Kill That Noise" in response to South Bronx. The album is produced by Marley Marl. It was the only Cold Chillin'/Warner Bros. album that was never initially released on CD by its distributor. The album was not released on that format until 1995, long after the 5-year distribution deal with Warner Bros. Records ended. By this time, Cold Chillin' distributed its material independently, mostly from its back catalog. This CD pressing would only be available for a limited time and went out of print for a few years. It was then re-released in 2001 as MC Shan: the Best of Cold Chillin', which featured all the tracks from Down by Law (except "Another One to Get Jealous Of") with a few additional non-album tracks.

TRACKS

"Jane, Stop This Crazy Thing!"

"Project Ho"

"The Bridge"

"Kill That Noise"

"Down by Law"

"Left Me Lonely"

"Another One to Get Jealous Of"

"MC Space"

"Living in the World of Hip-Hop"

"Beat Biter"

FOURTH ALBUM RELEASE BY WHODINI

'Open Sesame' was released in 1987 via Jive Records. Audio

production was handled almost entirely by Larry Smith, except for two tracks both produced by Sinister and Whodini. The record peaked at #30 on the Billboard 200, at #8 on the Top R&B/Hip-Hop Albums, and was certified gold by the Recording Industry Association of America on January 20, 1988.

Theo Huxtable Raps on The Cosby Show

By 1987, The Cosby Show had become one of the most successful television sitcoms in history, and handily the most successful sitcom with a predominantly African-American cast. Yet, the Cosby kids seemed to stay frozen in time, and run slightly awry of what actual kids their age were doing and saying. Those actual kids had their attention taken from them that Fall, though, when, during the fifth episode of the fourth season of "Cosby," Theo Huxtable and his friend Cockroach wrote a rap for a school assignment concerning the matter of Shakespeare's Julius Caesar.

In a show in which Bill Cosby had specifically avoided the (his words) "jive" parlance of the country's African-American youth, the sight of one of America's most famous teenagers rapping in their living rooms was a benchmark moment for kids and parents, further evidence to the entire country that rap wasn't just a passing fad in a small segment of the culture, but something that would be coming to all families, everywhere.

Theo set the foundation for characters like the Fresh Prince to arrive, but The Cosby Show remained generally conservative when it came to addressing hip-hop culture head-on for the rest of its run, which amounted to five more years, and totaled six seasons (or 202 episodes), and is generally considered one of the greatest family sitcoms of all time. Malcolm-Jamal Warner, who played Theo, has kept up with acting (and yes, in the '90s, dabbled in a brief music career that didn't exactly pop off).

1988

Geto Boys releases First Record

'Making Trouble' is the debut album by the Houston hip hop group the Geto Boys, then known as the Ghetto Boys. The group originally consisted of Bushwick Bill, DJ Ready Red, Sire Jukebox and Prince Johnny C. Following the release of Making Trouble, Rap-A-Lot Records dropped Sire Jukebox and Johnny C from the group, and added Scarface and Willie D. Making Trouble received little attention, and is often forgotten in the midst of the group's later successful, acclaimed and controversial albums.

TRACKS

"Making Trouble"

"Snitches"

"Balls and My Word"

"Assassins"

"Why Do We Live This Way"

"I Run This"

"No Curfew"

"One Time Freestyle"

"Geto Boys Will Rock You"

"You Ain't Nothin'"

"The Problem"

Biz Markie's releases his First Album

Goin' Off is the debut by hip-hop musician, Biz Markie. The album was released by Cold Chillin' Records, and produced by Marley Marl. The album was praised for its wit and humor. Big Daddy Kane wrote the lyrics of the album's first five songs. The album also showcased Biz's talent as a human beatbox on the song "Make the Music with Your Mouth, Biz", and his skill in the game of dozens on the track "Nobody Beats the Biz". One of his most widely known songs, "Vapors", was on the album.

Some reissues from 1995 onwards replace the Marley Marl

remix of "Make the Music with Your Mouth" with the original 12" version, the album version of "Vapors" with the remix, and the original "This Is Something for the Radio" with the remix. In 1998, the album was selected as one of The Source's 100 Best Rap Albums. In 2006, the album was re-released by Traffic Entertainment Group with a bonus disc. It restores the original album versions of "Vapors" and "This Is Something for the Radio" as well as the Marley Marl remix of "Make the Music" that appeared on the original LP.

DJ Jazzy Jeff and The Fresh Prince releases
second album

'He's the DJ, I'm the Rapper' was the first double album in hip hop music, in its original vinyl incarnation. The album's first single, "Brand New Funk", was only released promotionally and, thus, failed to achieve any commercial success. However, the album's second single, "Parents Just Don't Understand", won the first-ever Grammy Award for Best Rap Performance and reached number 12 on the Billboard Hot 100. Although the album's third single, "Nightmare on My Street", which reached number 15 on the Billboard Hot 100, was considered for inclusion in the movie A Nightmare on Elm Street 4: The Dream Master, the producers of the film decided against its inclusion. As a result, later vinyl pressings of the album contain a disclaimer sticker that says, *"[This song] is not part of the soundtrack and is not authorized, licensed, or affiliated with the Nightmare on Elm Street films."*

Boogie Down Productions' Second Album Release

'By All Means Necessary' was released on May 31, 1988 on Jive Records. After the 1987 murder of DJ-producer Scott La Rock, KRS-One moved away from the violent themes that dominated his debut, Criminal Minded, and began writing socially conscious songs using the moniker, "the Teacher." Many themes, which surface a minimalist production accompanied by hard-hitting drum beats, cover social issues that include government and police corruption, safe sex, government involvement in the drug trade, and violence in the hip-hop community.

TRACKS

"My Philosophy"

"Ya Slippin"

"Stop the Violence"

"Illegal Business"

"Nervous"

"I'm Still #1"

"Part Time Suckers"

"Jimmy"

"T'Cha-T'Cha"

"Necessary"

Doug E. Fresh Album #2

The World's Greatest Entertainer was released in 1988 on Reality Records, a short-lived subsidiary of Fantasy Records, and was produced by Doug E. Fresh, Eric "Vietnam" Sadler, Ollie Cotton and Carl Ryder. The album gained a fair amount of success, peaking at #88 on the Billboard 200 and #7 on the Top R&B/Hip-Hop Albums, and featured the single "Keep Risin' to the Top," which peaked at #4 on the Hot R&B/Hip-Hop Singles & Tracks.

TRACKS

"Guess? Who?"

"Every Body Got 2 Get Some"

"D.E.F. = Doug E. Fresh"

"On the Strength"

"Keep Risin' to the Top"

"Greatest Entertainer"

"I'm Gettin' Ready"

"Cut that Zero"

"The Plane (So High)"

"Ev'rybody Loves a Star"

"Crazy 'Bout Cars"

"Africa (Goin' back Home)"

Grandmaster Flash and the Furious Five releases second and Final Album

'On the Strength' was released in 1988, it was the full line-up's last album together. Although certainly contributing to the album itself, Cowboy (Keith Wiggins) was not present for the album or single photo shoots.

TRACKS

"Gold"

"Cold in Effect"

"Yo Baby"

"On the Strength"

"The King"

"Fly Girl"

"Magic Carpet Ride"

"Leave Here"

"This Is Where You Got It From"

"The Boy is Dope"

"Back in the Old Days of Hip-Hop"

<u>NEGLECTED BY THE MAINSTREAM MEDIA,
HIP-HOP GETS ITS OWN SHOW ON MTV,
"YO! MTV RAPS."</u>

Yo! MTV Raps is a two-hour American television music video program, which ran from August 1988 to August 1995. The program (created by Ted Demme and Peter Dougherty) was the first hip hop music show on the network, based on the original MTV Europe show, aired one year earlier. Yo! MTV Raps produced a mix of rap videos, interviews with rap stars, live in studio performances (on Fridays) and comedy. The show also yielded a Brazilian version called Yo! MTV and broadcast by MTV Brasil from 1990 to 2005. In 1987 Ted Demme and Peter Doughtery developed the program for the then nascent MTV Europe.

The year after that Run-DMC hosted the pilot episode in the US. Also featured in the pilot were DJ Jazzy Jeff & the Fresh Prince. Eric B. & Rakim's video for the title track of the album "Follow the Leader" was the first video to be shown on Yo! MTV Raps. The pilot was one of the highest rated programs to ever air on MTV at that point. Only the Video Music Awards and Live Aid received greater ratings. Shinehead's "Chain Gang" was the first video to be shown during a regular season episode. Meanwhile, Ice-T's "High Rollers" was the first video to be played during the weekday show. The classic Yo! MTV Raps logo was created by early graffiti writer, Dr. Revolt. The animated show open was produced by Nigel Cox-Hagen and animated by Beau Tardy.

Run–DMC releases fourth studio album

'Tougher Than Leather' was released on May 17, 1988. While the new record did not maintain the same popularity as its predecessor, it obtained platinum status and spawned the favorites "Run's House" and "Mary, Mary". Despite being given a mixed reception at the time of its release, it is now hailed as a seminal classic in hip-hop and many see it as an underrated album.

TRACKS

"Run's House"

"Mary, Mary"

"They Call Us Run-DMC"

"Beats To The Rhyme"

"Radio Station"

"Papa Crazy"

"Tougher Than Leather"

"I'm Not Going Out Like That"

"How'd Ya Do It Dee"

"Miss Elaine"

"Soul To Rock And Roll"

"Ragtime"

1989

LL Cool J's third album release

Walking with a Panther was released June 9, 1989, on Def Jam Recordings. While his previous album Bigger and Deffer (1987) was produced by The L.A. Posse, Dwayne Simon was the only member left of the group willing to work on 'Walking with a Panther', as other members, such as Bobby "Bobcat" Erving, wanted a higher pay after realizing how much of a success the previous album had become. Def Jam, however, refused to change the contract, which caused the L.A. Posse to leave. Walking with a Panther was primarily produced by LL Cool J and Dwayne Simon, with additional production from Rick Rubin and Public Enemy's production team, The Bomb Squad.

Gang Starr releases debut

'No More Mr. Nice Guy' was released on June 1989; and it peaked at #83 on the Billboard R&B chart. The song "Positivity" peaked at #19 on the Billboard rap chart. This album is one of the most unique collaborations between a DJ and Emcee.

TRACKS

"Premier & The Guru"

"Jazz Music"

"Gotch U"

"Manifest"

"Gusto"

"DJ Premier in Deep Concentration"

"Positivity (Remix)"

"Words I Manifest (Remix)"

"Conscience Be Free"

"Cause and Effect"

"2 Steps Ahead"

"No More Mr. Nice Guy"

"Knowledge"

"Positivity"

"Here's the Proof" (2001 Re-issue Bonus Track)

"The Lesson" (2001 Re-issue Bonus Track)

"Dedication" (2001 Re-issue Bonus Track)

Debut Album by Kool G Rap & DJ Polo

Road to the Riches was released in 1989 on then-prominent hip hop label Cold Chillin' Records. The album is notable in that it set off the mafioso rap trend with the title track "Road to the Riches," which received strong rotation on the TV show Yo! MTV Raps, and was later featured on the old-school hip hop radio station Playback FM from the game Grand Theft Auto: San Andreas. Most of the songs, however, are not crime-related. Other popular songs included "It's a Demo" and "Poison." In 1998, the album was selected as one of The Source's 100 Best Rap Albums.

Second studio album by the Houston's Geto Boys

"Grip It! On That Other Level" was released on March 12, 1989 on Rap-A-Lot Records. Following the disappointing results of the group's first album, Rap-A-Lot's CEO, James Prince replaced two of the group members with Scarface (then known as Akshen) and Willie D, who joined original members Bushwick Bill and DJ Ready Red. Recording for the album began in 1988, and finished in early 1989. The majority of the album's tracks were produced by DJ Ready Red, and much of the album's lyrical content deals with violent and misogynistic topics, which would later be credited for pioneering the horrorcore hip-hop subgenre.

Debut Album by American hip hop trio - De La Soul

'3 Feet High and Rising' was released on March 14, 1989, by Tommy Boy Records. It marked the first of three full-length collaborations with producer Prince Paul, which would become the critical and commercial peak of both parties. It is consistently placed on 'greatest albums' lists by noted music critics and publications. Robert Christgau called the record "unlike any rap album you or anybody else has ever heard." In 1998, the album was selected as one of The Source Magazine's 100 Best Rap Albums.

Critically, as well as commercially, the album was a success. It contains the singles, "Me Myself and I", "The Magic Number", "Buddy", and "Eye Know". In 2001, the album was re-issued along with an extra disc of B-side tracks, and alternative versions. The album title came from the Johnny Cash song "Five Feet High and Rising". It was selected by the Library of Congress as a 2010 addition to the National Recording Registry, which selects recordings annually that are culturally, historically, or aesthetically significant.

Audio Two hits the Hip-Hop Scene

What More Can I Say? is the debut studio album by hip-hop duo, Audio Two. It was released in 1988 through First Priority Records with distribution by Atlantic Records. Recording sessions took place at I.N.S. Studios, Such-A-Sound Studio and First Priority Lab in New York City. Production was handled by its members Milk Dee and DJ Gizmo with Daddy-O and the King of Chill. The album found only mild success, making it to #185 on the Billboard 200 and #45 on the Top R&B/Hip-Hop Albums chart in the United States. What More Can I Say? spawned four singles: "Make It Funky"/"Top Billin'", "Hickeys Around My Neck", "Many Styles"/"The Questions" and "I Don't Care". The song "I Like Cherries" was previously released on Flip-Flop Mini-Album, a 1986 split mini-LP dropped with the Alliance (King of Chill, Kool C and D.J. Dice).

D.O.C releases "No One Can Do It Better"

No One Can Do It Better is the debut studio album by The D.O.C., released on August 1, 1989 by Ruthless Records, and Atlantic Records. It reached number-one on the US Top R&B/Hip-Hop Albums chart for two weeks, while peaking in the Top 20 on the Billboard 200 chart.

The album was certified Gold by the RIAA three months after it was released, and Platinum on April 21, 1994. This was the only solo album The D.O.C. was able to record before a car accident resulted in crushing his larynx; in recent years, however, he has been undergoing vocal surgery. He would not release another album until 7 years later, with Helter Skelter (1996).

About The D.O.C

After Fila Fresh Crew split up in 1987, The D.O.C. went on to pursue a successful solo career. In 1989, he released his debut album, No One Can Do It Better, which reached number-one on the US Top R&B/Hip-Hop Albums chart for two weeks and spawned two number one hits on the Hot Rap Songs chart: "It's Funky Enough" and "The D.O.C. & The Doctor". The album went platinum five years after its release. In late 1989, months after the release of No One Can Do It Better, The D.O.C. suffered a serious car accident which resulted in the crushing of his larynx, permanently changing his voice. Since his recovery, he has released two more albums, Helter Skelter in 1996 and Deuce in 2003. Since 2006, The D.O.C. has been working on new material for his fourth album Voices. The D.O.C. continued to write for N.W.A and contributed lyrics and minor vocals to their final album "Niggaz4Life" and their 1990 EP "100 Miles and Runnin'", where he co-wrote all the songs except for "Just Don't Bite It" and "Kamurshol".

In 1991, The D.O.C left Ruthless Records along with Dr. Dre and Michel'le to sign with newly founded Death Row Records. Dr. Dre also used his talents as one of the writers for his debut solo album The Chronic, contributing to the tracks "Lil' Ghetto Boy", "A Nigga Witta Gun", and "Bitches Ain't Shit." He also appeared on the skit track "The $20 Sack Pyramid". He is referenced by name in "Nuthin' but a G Thang", and appears in the song's video as well. The liner notes to The Chronic say, "I want to give a special shout out to The D.O.C. for talking me into doin' this album." His name is mentioned by Snoop Dogg in the intro of the album *("Peace to da D.O.C., still makin' it funky enough")*.

VOLUME THREE

Hip-hop is the streets. Hip-hop is a couple of elements that it comes from back in the days... that feel of music with urgency that speaks to you. It speaks to your livelihood and it's not compromised. It's blunt. It's raw, straight off the street - from the beat to the voice to the words.

NAS

INTRODUCTION

These days, hip hop surrounds us really everywhere, whether it is on TV in the form of movies, music shows, or commercials, on the radio, or just in the streets, where various public places are aged-tagged, or when groups of young people make shows by breaking or rapping in front of randomly passing people in order to make some money, have fun and show what they can do. Shortly, nearly everyone has a certain idea about what is hip hop. It is such a complex area that includes music, dance, art such as graffiti, fashion, and many other fields which are connected with it, which still needs to be introduced and therefore the aim of this book is to make the further acquaintance of hip hop not only as a musical style, but as a whole phenomenon of hip hop culture which has been spreading among youth especially through the media across the whole world.

INTRODUCTION

Since its creation, Hip Hop has had a cultural impact on youth all around the world. The youth specifically because the music, for many, is a reflection of their lives and is told in a way they can easily understand. Beginning in the South Bronx of New York in November of 1974, Hip Hop consisted mainly of DJing, breaking (break dancing), graffiti, and rapping. However, it is much more than just a kind of music. Many believe that the genre can be seen as a way of life, given that it also has brought about new ways of dressing, expression, and its unique outlooks on cultural, political, economical and intellectual factors in society.

CHAPTER ONE
HIP HOP AT A GLANCE

There are several mistakes that circulate among people. For example, a lot of people think hip hop is only a musical style and that hip hop and rap is the same thing. Therefore, I would like to explain some terms that are concerned with hip hop at the beginning of this essay.

Firstly, hip hop is not only a musical style, it includes a large number of areas, and music is just one of them. It is quite difficult to define hip hop because of its complexity, but there are several definitions of this phenomenon such as a US pop culture movement originating in the 1980s comprising rap music, graffiti and break dancing" or a popular urban youth culture, closely associated with rap music and with the style and fashions of African-American inner-city residents, the most precious definition of hip hop can be found in Martin Fiedler's Hip hop Forever: "Hip hop is a lifestyle with a developed and colorful culture, its language, and fashion style, specific kind of music and thinking, which is constantly developing."

Another interesting opinion of what hip hop is, belongs to DJ and MC TC Izlam, who claims: "Hip hop is just a way of thinking, state of mind. To be a hip-hopper means to think freely." The second mistake that hip hop and rap can be used synonymously is also very common among people who do not understand this issue. From the definitions that are mentioned above is clear what hip hop means. Rap is "a rhythmic monologue with musical backing, "which means that it's just a lexical part of hip hop music which is just one of the several parts of whole hip hop culture.

The name "Hip Hop" is said to have been coined by Keith "Cowboy" Wiggins. Wiggins was a member of Grandmaster Flash and the Furious Five, a Hip-Hip group formed in 1978 in the South Bronx. They were a large part of the genre's earliest pioneers. Other artists signifying the beginning of Hip Hop include The Sugar Hill Gang. Signed by Sylvia Robinson, they have been recognized as the first popular rap group. Their song, "Rapper's Delight," is still popular today. The first female group to release a Hip Hop single was known as The Sequence, releasing "Funk You Up" in 1979 while the first female solo artist to do so was Lady B in the same year.

CHAPTER TWO
REVIEW OF THE ELEMENTS OF HIP HOP

We wrote on this topic in our second volume of the History of Hip Hop and is listing again to give background to those who are new to the series.

Hip hop culture contains four essential elements: DJing, MCing, graffiti art and b-boying. DJing and MCing symbolize a musical part, b-boying stands for a dance component, and graffiti represents a visual art constituent of this culture. Of course, these four elements did not originate at the same time, but their combination enabled hip hop to come into existence.

DJing

DJing is a fundamental means to produce hip hop music. The DJ is the abbreviation for the phrase 'disc jockey' – a person, who plays recorded, not live, music or sound for an audience. The very first disc jockeys were radio DJs, who played the music to radio listeners and in the 1950s, DJs started to perform "live" at various parties. Americans were always used to dancing at a bar to music from a jukebox, but paying for a DJ not playing "live" music was not very common.

In 1973, DJ Kool Herc took two turntables, which he connected to a mixer and he laid two identical records on the turntables. The mixer helps DJ in the smooth transition of sound from one turntable to the second one. Kool Herc played a break of one record and the same break of the second record, which he could easily repeat. This method is known as "mixing breaks"6 or "creating breakbeats"7. Herc played the music for an audience of dancers who are known as b-boys, or break boys, and b-girls or break girls. Under the influence of DJ Kool Herc, some of the b-boys such as Grandmixer DXT and Kurtis Blow became DJs too. Herc contributed to the development of DJing by creating a huge mobile sound system, because he knew how to connect more speakers and generate more electrical power to be able to make a louder sound. Another innovative DJ was Grandmaster Flash, who brought to perfection the Herc's way of mixing two records. He developed a theory called a "quick mix theory," which is based upon marking records and using a headset to be able to hear how is the second record combined with the first one before the audience can hear it via the loudspeaker and make a fluent transition from one record to the other.

Grand Wizard Theodore, a pupil of Grandmaster Flash,

accidentally created a technique of DJing called "scratching." One day of the year 1975, when he was improving his DJing skills at home, his mother told him to turn down the volume. Because he did not hear it, she entered his room and he tried to stop the music by laying his hand on the playing record to stop its spinning. By moving it back and forward to keep the record quiet and be able to listen to his mother's words, he noted that this movement creates a unique sound. It is necessary to mention that this technique is commonly used by DJs up to this day.

In the mid-1990s came to the rise of the turntablism movement, which caused the DJing became again one of the essential elements of Hip Hop. It was a new generation of DJs, who wanted to regain the dominant role of the DJ in the music and make the turntable to be a musical instrument again. The advances in technology in the twenty-first century moved DJing to the next level. Because of digital technology, DJs are allowed to play music through digital music files saved in notebooks or the use of CD players. These technological advances allow almost everyone to become a DJ because DJs do not need to have a wide collection of records anymore, which require a lot of space and also can be expensive.

Over time, DJs started to use microphones and talk to their audiences to keep them interested and MCs took the role later.

. . .

MCing

MCing is often used as a synonym for rapping, but it is just one part of what an MC does. The MC is the acronym of the phrase 'master of ceremonies and over time, the title MC began to be used as an abbreviation for phrases such as 'microphone controller' or 'microphone checker'. The role of MC is the assistance to DJ in keeping the audience excited and entertained and encouraging b-boys and b-girls to dance. To be an MC provided an opportunity to express one's feelings and opinions of society and the environment in which one lives. Coke La Rock, who cooperated with DJ Kool Herc, was the first significant hip hop MC. In the mid-1970s, MCs were not only helpers of DJs, but they became their partners. From the combination of DJ and MC evolved a large number of groups. The advances in technology changed the relationship between DJ and MC. Thanks to the digital audiotape and the cassette, MCs of the 1980s were able to perform without the presence of DJs because they could play recorded music through these cassettes and tapes. The value of MCs also rose in the eyes of record labels, who sought out talented MCs such as KRS-One, Kurtis Blow, Queen Latifah or Rakim. Thanks to them, MCs became hip hop superstars and icons of popular culture. The growing importance of MCs caused that they gained the success and grabbed all the money.No wonder that MCs became so significant in hip hop culture when they are supposed to have several skills to be able to fulfill their roles. MCs have a high degree of originality and versatility; attain a high level of mastery over substance, flow, and 'battle skills'; have a significant social impact, and possess outstanding live performance abilities."

B-boying

B-boying is a kind of street dance and it is often called 'breakdancing' or 'breaking'. It was inspired by dance elements of other dance styles that already existed, but breakers except that they adapt old moves also invent a large number of new ones. It is a very difficult kind of dance and keeping balance and being flexible play an important role when doing the breaking. History of b-boying goes back to the 1970s when each gang contained a crew of dancers. The old-school rap historians claim that "the first break dancers were... street gang members who danced upright."10 These dancers were predominantly African American and they took breaking only as a way of dancing. The question is, whether breaking would have still existed if Hispanic teenagers had not become excited about it. It was the Hispanics, who brought competitiveness into b-boying. Crews of b-boys and b-girls dared other breakers to meet them at a specific place, where they created a circle in which pairs of dancers alternate in dancing, till one of the dance crews are recognized as the winning one. In 1982, b-boying/b-girling got to the mainstream by performing of Rock Steady Crew on ABC News, where they battled against the Dynamic Rockers. Among the fundamental techniques of b-boying belong toprock, uprock, downrock, power moves, and freeze.

Other Elements

Over time, as hip hop was rising and spreading, another element began to enter the hip hop culture. In the 1980s, Afrika Bambaataa, one of the excellent DJs, tried to enforce a fifth element that was called "Knowledge, Culture and Overstanding. It consisted of comprehending the principles laid by the hip hop pioneers and the conceptual history of the preceding elements. The term "overstanding" contained a positivist ideology taken from Rastafarianism, which emphasized a superior positive power, not on the negative one. Others wanted "beatboxing," which is vocal percussion imitating various musical sounds and instruments, to be the fifth element, but it continues to be an underground phenomenon within hip hop culture. In the 1980s, as hip hop became national music, the people listening to this kind of music needed to identify with it by selecting a particular kind of clothes. Clothing companies and shoe manufacturers such as Adidas, Nike, and Timberland gave them this opportunity. This specific clothing includes pieces such as saggy pants, oversized T-shirts, hooded coats and sweatshirts, and hip hop caps. Because hip hop culture arose and evolved on the street, a particular language style is an integral part of it. It is the slang, because of which hip hop has often been criticized, but as hip hop became mainstream, a lot of expressions got into wider society and also current dictionaries. For example in the Oxford English Dictionary, we can find a definition of the noun and the adjective bling bling, which sounds: "denoting expensive, ostentatious clothing or jewelry, or the style or materialistic attitudes associated with them." It is important to mention that the four basic elements did not arise along with hip hop. They existed independently of it, but their combination enabled the birth of this culture.

CHAPTER THREE
ELEMENTS OF B-BOYING

Toprock

Toward the beginning of b-boying, breakdance was about the toprock. It is the most basic procedure, which incorporates a wide range of moves done in a standing position. Toprock is normally the initial step of a dancer, who at that point continues going downwards. A b-boy historian called Jorge "Popmaster Fabel" Pabon says about the beginnings of breaking: "It was all carefully top-shaking, intriguing drops to get down to the floor, incredible blitz-speed footwork. It was entirely unpredictable. Bouncing around, rotating, turning, turns, front-clears, you know? What's more, aggressive, extremely aggressive, to the point that I thought it was a gang dance at first."

· · ·

Uprock

This technique arose before b-boying itself, just to be more specific, it came into existence in Brooklyn during the 1960s. When breakers were doing uprock, "rivals lined up across each other, and went head-to-head – making as if they were jigging, stabbing, battering each other." The uprock style requires two rival breakers or crews who dance toprock alternatively whole time the song is playing. It looks like the dancers were fighting with each other, but there is not any physical contact allowed in this dance. The winning dancer or crew is the one that shows better and faster dance elements and combinations.

Downrock

The downrock is a dance technique which is also called "footwork". The pioneer of this style was the crew called Rock Steady Crew, which was established in the South Bronx in 1977. It describes all kinds of movements which are performed on the floor and the emphasis is put especially on feet, but hands are commonly used to support the dancer. The 6-step is the basic move of the downrock and it simply reminds of walking in a circle on the floor with one hand touching the ground. Except for the use of feet and hands, the legs and knees can be also involved in performing this technique

. . .

Power Moves

The power moves are more complex even acrobatic breaking moves that sometimes remind of gymnastics rather than a dance. This technique is very difficult and requires a great deal of speed, momentum, strength, and endurance. The power moves include moves like the windmill, headspin, backspin, or flare. When doing the windmill, breaker spins on the floor, from his back to his chest and back again, and his legs move in the air in a V-shape. There are many starting positions and also many variations of this move. The headspin is a kind of power move in which the dancer rotates on his head often using a cap. During performing this technique is required to be able to keep a perfect balance of the whole body, especially the legs. It is usually performed without any other support, but the use of hands to keep or gain the speed is described as "tapping".

Freeze

The freeze technique is commonly used to end a power move. It is kind of a pose when the dancer puts his body into a unique position usually holding on his hands and simply stops. There is probably an infinite number of variations of this technique, which is strongly connected to the rhythm of the music. Primarily b-boying took credit for the birth of hip hop because it was the b-boys and b-girls who were the inspiration for DJ Kool Herc in creating the breakbeat. Nevertheless, b-boying or b-girling will probably never be as much important and prominent again as in the era of early hip hop.

CHAPTER FOUR
ELEMENTS OF GRAFFITI CULTURE

Nelson George in Hip Hop America writes that "graffiti has been around since man encountered his first stone wall." It is true that graffiti has been in existence for centuries, but this kind of graffiti has nothing in common with hip hop culture. The style of graffiti that is liked to hip hop was born in Philadelphia the end of the 1960s, where graffiti writers such as Cornbread, Cool Earl and Top Cat had been painting the walls since 1967. This modern graffiti art is also called 'writing' or 'aerosol art'.

The term 'tag' referring to the graffiti is commonly used among graffiti artists and it stands for new names, which artists gave themselves in order to protect them from revelation. A verb 'to tag' was derived from this noun and it means 'to paint' or 'to mark'. The tagging is concerned not only with painting walls, but also buses, trains, subway cars and stations, and many other places in cities. In 1970, a

Greek-American teenager started to tag his nickname "TAKI 183" in subway stations of Manhattan because graffiti was so widespread there. In the very same year, the New York Times described "TAKI 183" as the creator of the graffiti phenomenon in New York City.

There are many styles of graffiti around the world. The best-known styles such as tag style, throw-up, wild style, and others will be introduced in the following paragraphs.

Tag style

This style is also called "tagging" and it is the oldest of all graffiti techniques. It is a writer's signature depicted on the streets' walls or in public places to be seen by as many people as possible. To be able to perform this technique one needs just a marker. The main representative of this style was already mentioned TAKI 183. From the beginning, it was just a regular signature, but today, when graffiti is more developed, every writer has its style of writing.

Simple style

It is the basic technique and the first step for a beginning writer. Separately written letters of simple shape are characteristic for this style, in which the basic task is to create one's style and improve one's skills because the letters should have a form of a certain style without any additional elements. This technique is often used by writers when writing a longer text or creating a signature.

Throw-up style

This technique is more advanced than tagging. The throw-ups usually consist of two colors and they are created through the use of spray paint. Throw- up letters have a shape similar to bubbles or even clouds. This technique is often used in "bombing," which means tagging a large number of areas in a night, or when writers want to cover previous works of other artists. The advantage of the throw-up style is that it is very easy and quick to do; it means that it could be done in one stroke and two minutes or less.

Blockbuster style

The title of this graffiti technique describes the way how letters are written. A blockbuster picture consists of big and square letters and usually of two colors. It is also used to cover earlier works of another artist and this style has the advantage of being easy to write and also easy to read. It is possible to see it on cars, trains, or in places with plenty of space to be able to write the letters nice, big and readable. Because of quite clearly defined square letters, there are not many possibilities how to be creative, and therefore there did not occur any significant changes in this style.

• • •

Wild style

The wild style is considered to be one of the most difficult techniques. It is a style of complicated, abstract, and very colorful pictures with various additional elements like spikes, arrows and many others. It depends on the writer's own imagination, how the paint will look like. The paintings consist of letters of a certain style, which can drive off in various directions and are connected in some way. It is usually very hard to read paints in this style for the wide public and therefore it is intended especially, but not exclusively, for her graffiti writers, who can without too much trouble decipher these paints based on the connections between letters. Semi-wild style is a kind of wild style graffiti, which is very popular with graffiti writers and the hip hop community. It is very much like wild style, but it is readable and not so time- consuming to paint.

3D Style

The 3D style graffiti is completely different from the other techniques. It is also a very complicated technique with an amazing three-dimensional effect by which shadows play the key role. To be able to do 3D graffiti, a writer needs to know how light and shadows work together. In Martin Fiedler's Hip Hop Forever is stated that "this technique is highly controversial." The problem is that there are writers who think that 3D style is the cream of the graffiti art, and on the other hand, there are writers who do not consider the 3D graffiti artists like writers, but painters. The process of becoming a graffiti writer is difficult and takes a long time. In the beginning, one has to pick a nickname, create one's tag and then it is possible to learn other techniques and develop a personal style. It is also important to learn how to use and apply spray paint and adhere to certain rules concerning graffiti. The process of creating a graffiti painting also is not as easy as it may seem. It includes a lot of effort and imagination of writers, who usually create a sketch before they go tagging. Graffiti is still highly controversial today. On the one hand, a lot of people think that graffiti is just vandalism because it is possible to see a large number of public places that are tagged. On the other hand, there are people who consider graffiti as art and visit galleries and various expositions for that.

CHAPTER FIVE
1990S

In the 80s, hip-hop firmly established itself as both a cultural and commercially viable force; it was still primarily an underground concern. The following decade changed all that. Not only did hip-hop hit arguably its artistic high, but, for the first time, its artists became superstars in their own right. The huge hits of 90s hip-hop put the genre firmly at the top of the heap – a lofty position from which it's never looked back. At the dawn of the 90s, hip-hop faced something of a crisis. The success of gangsta rap groups such as Los Angeles natives NWA, whose 1988 debut album, Straight Outta Compton, detailed street violence in an uncompromising and explicit style, led to many radio stations pulling effective boycotts against hip-hop's more aggressive artists. To make matters worse, Gilbert O'Sullivan's successful court case against Biz Markie, in 1991 (he'd used a sample of O'Sullivan's 'Alone

Again (Naturally)' without consent), threatened to change the very way the art form was constructed; no longer could producers use multiple samples, for fear of litigation. On the plus side, artistically, hip-hop was in rude health. The first few years of the decade saw 90s hip-hop classics from the likes of Public Enemy (Fear Of A Black Planet), A Tribe Called Quest (Peoples Instinctive Travels And The Paths Of Rhythm, The Low-End Theory), De La Soul (De La Soul Is Dead) and Main Source (Breaking Atoms). NWA's 1991 follow-up, Efil4zaggin, showed the tables were beginning to turn commercially. The album moved way beyond its urban heartland and into the bedrooms of suburban youth, becoming the first album by a hip-hop group to hit No.1 on the Billboard 200. By that point, however, the group had started to disintegrate. Ice Cube had left in acrimonious fashion the previous year (releasing his debut solo album, AmeriKKKa's Most Wanted, to critical and commercial success), followed by Dr. Dre, whose own solo career would change the course of hip-hop history.

Forming Death Row Records with Suge Knight and The DOC, Dre used the fledgling imprint to issue his stratospherically popular debut album, The Chronic, at the tail-end of 1992. His revolutionary production style – christened G-Funk – was a canny mix of deep rolling bass, P-Funk-indebted grooves and soulful vocals that smoothed the jagged edges of gangsta rap into a more accessible format which radio stations could get behind. With Death

Row Records releasing a succession of hugely successful G-Funk records by artists such as Tha Dogg Pound (Dogg Food) and Snoop Dogg (whose 1993 debut album, Doggystyle, entered the Billboard charts at No.1), 90s hip-hop saw the West Coast usurp its Eastern counterpart as the dominant force in rap music, its artists becoming huge stars and establishing themselves as part of the mainstream.

However, while New York was struggling to compete commercially, its scene was far from stagnant. 1993 saw the release of A Tribe Called Quest's incandescent third album, Midnight Marauders, and the arrival of Wu-Tang Clan, whose groundbreaking debut album, Enter The Wu-Tang: 36 Chambers, heralded a new era for gritty East Coast hip-hop. The following year was just as strong for local talent, with Nas releasing his monumental debut, Illmatic, and Notorious BIG issuing his first, hugely successful, solo venture, Ready To Die. Released on Sean Combs' Bad Boy Entertainment label, that album's hit singles 'Juicy', 'Big Poppa' and 'One More Chance' (which matched Michael Jackson's 'Scream' for the highest-ever debut on the pop charts), led to the album shifting over four million units, turning Biggie into a major star.

The rivalry between the two coasts' hip-hop scenes was, however, far from healthy. In 1995, one of LA's biggest stars, 2Pac, was shot by a pair of muggers while in New York, the day before being found guilty of sexual assault. While in prison, he later accused Sean Combs and former friend Notorious BIG, among others, of being behind the shooting. Suge Knight, who would bail 2Pac out of prison later that year before signing the rapper to Death Row, joined the fray when he publicly insulted Sean Combs on stage at The Source Awards.

2Pac's law-breaking notoriety hadn't done his career any harm, and by the middle of the decade he was not only one of 90s hip-hop's biggest stars, but one of the most bankable acts in music. Released in 1995, while the rapper was still in prison, Me Against The World reached No.1 on the Billboard charts, while the following year he released All Eyez On Me, his first album for Death Row. An astonishing double-album (hip-hop's first) tour de force, All Eyez On Me confirmed 2Pac's status as one of the genre's most singular voices as well as one of its most successful, again hitting No.1, and shifting 566,000 copies in its first week. The simmering feud which had been building between Death Row and Bad Boy ended tragically. Leaving a Mike Tyson fight in Las Vegas, on 7 September 1996, a car carrying 2Pac and Suge Knight was peppered with bullets. Six days later, 2Pac died from his injuries. The following year, Notorious BIG shared an eerily similar fate after he was shot and killed in a drive-by shooting. While Biggie's Life After Death album, released just a few days after, became the best-selling hip-hop album of all time, the genre was forced to do some serious soul-searching in its wake.

Sean Combs was the first to point the route towards a less

opposing fine art. Soon thereafter, like Puff Daddy, he discharged two benefit singles in memory of his killed companion. His following hit-laden solo career, different enterprising interests and prominent relationship with Jennifer Lopez made him a standout amongst the most conspicuous figures to rise up out of 90s hip-hop, foretelling another age of rap stars who were as agreeable on celebrity lane or in the meeting room as they were in the account studio. Big deal's protégé, Jay Z, additionally proceeded onward from the clear brutality of his 1995 debut, Reasonable Doubt. 1997's In My Lifetime, bridled Sean Combs and Teddy Riley's radio-accommodating preparations to traverse into the pop market. Joined with his acclaimed rapping prowess, the album – and its hit-laden 1998 successor, Hard Knock Life, slung Jay Z to the genius status he proceeds to hold.

There was one increasingly seismic move in hip-hop before the decade was out. Dr. Dre, who, in 1996, had surrendered Death Row to set up his new steady, Aftermath Entertainment, marked a then little-known Detroit rapper, Eminem, to the name. The following 1999 album, The Marshall Mathers LP, beat the charts. Establishing 90s hip-hop as the point of worldwide strength for the music, the album likewise put Eminem on his way to turning into the top-selling craftsman in music, guaranteeing that hip-hop's very own direction would keep on taking off in the decades that followed. While hip-hop has appreciated various brilliant years, none was as earth-shattering as the 1990s. Rap music both overwhelmed the charts and thrived in the underground, while the establishments for present-day urban music were likewise mapped out. Things could never be the equivalent again. Here are the key factors behind the 1990s case to being the decade in hip-hop history.

NOTORIOUS BIG'S LIFE AFTER DEATH CEMENTS HIS REPUTATION AS THE GREATEST OF ALL TIME

Biggie's gangsta-fied '94 debut, Ready To Die, might have brought East Coast hip-hop back to prominence, but it was its follow-up that confirmed him as an all-time great. Puff Daddy's smooth and soulful productions proved the perfect foil for Biggie's ingenious lyrical turns and charismatic, a smooth-as-silk flow which set a benchmark for MCing that has yet to be bettered. Tragically, it was to prove his swansong. Shot and killed while leaving a party in Los Angeles

JAY Z HONOURS BIGGIE'S LEGACY, PICKS UP THE MANTLE OF GREATEST RAPPER ALIVE WITHIN MY LIFETIME

Hit hard by Biggie's passing, close friend Jay Z toned down the gangsta posturing on his sophomore effort. With Puff Daddy's production team, The Hitmen crafting a pop-leaning, soul-inflected backdrop, Hova delivered a jaw-dropping series of performances that confirmed him as a worthy heir apparent to the throne of the greatest earning rapper. A substantial hit at the time, (the album debuted at No. 3 in the Billboard charts), its savvy mix of tough posturing and pop nous provided the template that would see Jay ultimately become one of the music world's biggest stars.

MISSY ELLIOTT CHARTS HIP-HOP'S FUTURE WITH SUPA DUPA FLY

Refusing to be confined by genre conventions, Missy grabbed hip-hop and R&B by the horns on her debut album. Backed by a youthful Timbaland, whose spare, digital funk and skittery beats added a space-age sheen, Missy's staccato raps, and soulful vocals delivered rhymes that were at once humorous, assertive, intelligent, unique and unforgettable. With Timbaland's productions providing the template for much of the next decade's urban music, Missy forged a revolutionary path for female artists that would be later followed by the likes of Nicky Minaj.

COMPANY FLOW REIGNITE HIP-HOP'S UNDERGROUND WITH FUNCRUSHER PLUS

Despite only releasing one album proper, Company Flow had a stratospheric impact on the hip-hop underground. Angry, defiantly independent and determined to push rap's envelope with their uncompromising approach to production and lyrical flow, they laid the groundwork for the boldly experimental music that was to follow in its wake. Co Flow main man El-P is still going strong with his Run The Jewels project, while the release also served to put one of the greatest label's in hip-hop history, Rawkus, on the map. Company Flow reignites hip-hop's underground with Funcrusher Plus.

SLUM VILLAGE'S DEBUT ALBUM INTRODUCES J DILLA AS HIP-HOP'S GREATEST PRODUCER

While Dilla had been steadily building his reputation since '95 with stellar productions for the likes of A Tribe Called Quest, Janet Jackson and The Pharcyde, it wasn't until he formed Slum Village, with rappers T3 and Baatin, that the world was able to enjoy a full album of his warm, soulful and superlatively percussive productions. Bootlegged at the time (it wasn't given a full release until years later), Fan-Tas-Tic has had a lasting impact on a generation of producers.

WU-TANG CLAN BREAK SALES RECORDS WITH WU-TANG FOREVER

Any lingering worries record companies may have had about hip-hop's long-term commercial viability must surely have been quelled by the astronomical success of the Wu's sophomore effort. Despite being two hours in length, and prefaced by the similarly unwieldy 'Triumph' single, the Wu's masterplan of releasing multiple solo albums over the previous five years had paid off, as Wu-Tang Forever sold by the bucket-load, becoming the first rap album to debut at Number on both the US and UK mainstream charts

CHAPTER SIX
HIP HOP HISTORY (1990-1999)

- Ice Cube takes his new crew, Da Lench Mob to New York and records his solo debut with production from The Bomb Squad, Public Enemy's team of producers. The album, "AmeriKKKa's Most Wanted," is praised by the hip-hop community as a classic and sets Cube on the road to solo super stardom.

- Another addition to the (ever-growing) Native Tongues family, Queens-based A Tribe Called Quest to release their debut album, "People's Instinctive Travels and the Paths of Rhythm." Building on the template established by the Jungle Brothers, Queen Latifah, and, most notably, De La Soul; the group is praised for its intelligently quirky lyrics and inventive musical style.

- M.C. Hammer continues his pop-rap reign with his two Grammy nominations, a new Saturday morning cartoon, and an action figure. Despite all of his commercial success; there is a growing backlash against his image and music among rap fans and artists.

- Salt-N-Pepa release their third album, "Blacks Magic." The album receives the strongest reviews of their career; with the single 'Let's Talk About Sex' being especially praised for it's honest and thoughtful look at relationships and promiscuity.

- After shooting his cousin and leading police on a high-speed chase, Slick Rick is captured and taken to prison. Def Jam head Russell Simmons bails Rick out in time to finish his second album, "The Ruler's Back," but Rick is eventually sentenced to five years in prison on charges of attempted murder

- A video showing four L.A. police officers brutally beating a Black man named Rodney King is played at news stations all over the country. Several rappers contend that this has been happening for years in inner cities and call for change.

- M.C. Hammer releases his third proper album,

"2 Legit To Quit." Although the title cut is a sizeable hit; the album fails to match the across-the-board success of its predecessor as the backlash against 'pop-rap' has Hammer losing his (already limited) credibility among rap fans and the general public.

- Dr. Dre; citing a dispute over finances with Eazy-E and Ruthless Records; quits N.W.A. Dre is still under contract to Ruthless; and hires gangster-turned-businessman Marion "Suge" Knight to get him out of his deal with the record label. With Dre departing for a solo career, N.W.A. officially split.

- Sean Combs, still only 20 years old, is promoted to A&R at Uptown Records and executive produces hit albums for Father MC and Heavy D.

- Alternative rap group Main Source release their debut, the critically acclaimed "Breaking Atoms." While it doesn't sell very well, the group becomes among hip-hop's most respected, and the single, 'Live At the Bar-B-Q' features a memorable verse by a seventeen-year-old Queens rapper named Nas.

- 2Pac Shakur, former roadie, dancer, and second-string MC for Digital Underground, releases his debut album, "2Pacalypse Now." It immediately incites controversy for its content; particular lyrics regarding police officers. Vice President Dan Quayle even calls for a ban of the album during his campaign for re-election. Shakur's visibility is also raised by a star-making performance in the gritty urban drama "Juice".

- Body Count; Ice-T's new rap-metal band, release their debut album. The song 'Cop Killa' ignites a fire storm of controversy for it's lyrics about killing police officers. After nationwide protests from law enforcement officials, Time-Warner pressures Ice-T to pull the song from the album and eventually sells its share of Interscope Records, the distributor.

- With "Paul's Boutique" obtaining cult-classic status in the years following it's release; the Beastie Boys third album, "Check Your Head," becomes a smash hit, debuting in the Top Ten and returning the Boys to the charts for the first time since their debut album - although with a much different sound.

- After producing a successful album for R&B singer Mary J. Blige and remixing several other hits for artist such as Jodeci and Heavy D., Sean "Puffy" Combs is fired from Uptown after a dispute with label head Andre Harrell. Snoop Doggy Dogg releases the short film/soundtrack, "Murder Was the Case". With it's graphic storytelling about a man being sentenced for murder uncomfortably close to Snoop's real-life legal woes, many critics blast the rapper for exploiting the unfortunate circumstances.

- "southernplayalisticadillacmuzik," the debut album from Atlanta-based rap duo Outkast signals a shift from hip-hop's bi-coastal grip. Loose and funky with clever lyrics and insightful subject-matter, the group becomes a cult favorite among hip-hop enthusiasts.

- Adding to a seemingly endless string of legal charges, 2Pac is charged with sexual assault by a female fan in New York City.

- Bone Thugs-N-Harmony; a new Cleveland-based rap group discovered by Eazy-E; release an EP called "Creepin' On Ah Come-up." Their sound is a combination of rapid-fire speed-rapping and vocal harmonizing and the single, "Thuggish Ruggish Bone" becomes a moderate hit.

- Notorious B.I.G., after cameo appearances on several popular singles, finally releases "Ready to Die," his debut album for Bad Boy. It spawns two hit singles, 'Juicy' and 'Big Poppa;' one hit remix, 'One More Chance,' and returns the East Coast to the top of the charts after a two-year absence. It also elevates Puffy Combs' Bad Boy label to the top of hip-hop.

- Jay-Z's debut album, "Reasonable Doubt" is released to much praise from critics. Despite all of the accolades, it barely makes a dent on the charts.

- After leaving a Mike Tyson fight in Las Vegas, Nevada; a car carrying Suge Knight and Tupac Shakur is riddled with gunfire. Though Suge only suffers minor injuries, 2Pac--after fighting for his life for seven days in a hospital--dies from his wounds. The hip-hop nation goes into shock and mourning for the fallen rapper.

- Southern rap duo Outkast release their second album, "ATLiens." It is critically acclaimed for its positive outlook, progressive lyrics and a more futuristic production style.

- The Notorious B.I.G. is almost killed in a car accident in New Jersey. With his leg partially shattered, he is forced to walk with a cane. After a year of critical acclaim, The Fugees announce that they are going their separate ways; citing creative differences. Wyclef Jean almost immediately begins work on his solo debut.

- After leaving the Soul Train Music Awards in Los Angeles, the Notorious B.I.G. is shot and killed in a drive-by shooting that eerily resembles what happened to 2Pac six months earlier. With the twin murders of two of it's biggest stars, the hip-hop nation is forced to take stock of itself and what it represents. B.I.G.'s second album, the prophetically titled "Life After Death," is released only a few days after his killing and becomes the best-selling rap album of all time.

- Sean Combs, now calling himself 'Puff Daddy' releases two benefit singles as memoriam to the slain Notorious B.I.G.

- The Wu-Tang Clan release their second album, the double LP "Wu-Tang Forever." It sells well, but fails to match the critical respect of the group's more acclaimed debut.

- Suge Knight is sentenced to four years in prison for parole violation.

- After writing and producing hits for MC Lyte and R&B groups Xscape and 702; female rap artist Missy "Misdemeanor" Elliott releases her debut album, "Supa Dupa Fly." It is an artistic triumph and she is praised for her wit and quirky musical approach.

- Puff Daddy makes his debut as an artist with "No Way Out." Spawning four top ten singles, the album becomes a monster hit and makes Puffy the biggest star on the Bad Boy label in the wake of B.I.G.'s murder.

- Snoop Doggy Dogg finally releases his second album, the lackluster "The Doggfather." After the album fails to sell, Snoop announces he is leaving the crumbling Death Row Records.

- After starring in his third-straight summer blockbuster, "Men In Black"; Will Smith confirms his status as one of the biggest box-office draws of the 90s. In a somewhat surprising move, he also returns to music, releasing his first solo album, "Big Willie Style." Though lightweight, it becomes one of the best-selling albums of the year.

- East Coast Queensbridge, NY rappers begin to take over gangsta' rap; led by Nas (Illmatic) Mobb Deep (Shook Ones) along with Large Professor, Tragedy, Big Noyd and others from the Borough

- Ending a five-year period of seclusion that saw his

VOLUME THREE

reputation as a lyricist reach near-mythic proportions; Rakim finally makes his return with "The 18th Letter," his solo debut.

- Def Squad dominates after EPMD's split. Redman, K-Solo, Jamal, Keith Murray takes over and their hits filled ears worldwide

- After operating in obscurity in the Deep South for almost a decade, New Orleans based rapper-entrepreneur Master P releases "Ghetto D." Derided by critics as an untalented hack; the album nonetheless becomes a hit and opens the floodgates for a wealth of New Orleans gangsta rap to hit the airwaves. Master P, as founder and CEO of the No Limit record label, unexpectedly becomes one of the most powerful men in hip-hop.

- Picking up where the Notorious B.I.G. left off (at least commercially), new Bad Boy rapper Ma$e releases his debut album, "Harlem World." It is a smash and confirms Bad Boy's status as the (now undisputed) top label in rap.

- Def Jam Records signs Jay-Z and releases popular albums by rappers Redman, Method Man, and Foxy Brown; signalling a return to form for Russell Simmons and rap's longest-running label.

- Simmons also signs a newly-reformed EPMD and DMX, an intense MC from Yonkers. Jay-Z releases his second album, "In My Lifetime." It sells much better than his debut, but critics deride it as a flaky attempt to reach a crossover audience.

- Afeni Shakur, mother of the slain 2Pac Shakur; releases "R U Still Down (Remember Me)," a double-album of unreleased material the rapper recorded before his death. It is the beginning of a flood of songs, compilations and albums from the deceased rap star's vaults.

- DMX makes his debut with "It's Dark and Hell Is Hot" and intensely personal album of hard-core rap and poignant confessionals. It becomes a monster hit and signals a return of gritty, hard-core rap after a year of the more radio-friendly, Bad Boy-influenced party-rap.

- Master P's No Limit Records continues to churn out one hit album after the other; even though critics and hip-hop purists scoff at the cheap production and lackluster artists on the label. Seeking to strike while he's hot, P also creates No Limit Films, No Limit Wireless, and his own Percy Miller Clothing Line.

- Jay-Z's third album,: Hard Knock Life," becomes

his biggest-seller and restores some of his credibility in hip-hop circles. He immediately is heralded as the biggest rapper in hip-hop.

- Lauryn Hill, formerly of the Fugees; releases her solo debut, "The Miseducation of Lauryn Hill." With an emphasis on confessional songwriting and a powerful mix of rap, reggae, gospel, soul and folk, it becomes the most-acclaimed album of the year and thrusts Hill into international stardom.

- "Aquemini;" the third outing for Atlanta rappers Outkast; is a startling leap forward for the group. Combining live instruments with thought-provoking and forward-thinking lyrics, as well as meshing hip-hop, country, soul, techno, and funk elements, the album follows Lauryn Hill's debut as one of the most acclaimed albums of the year, though it isn't as successful commercially.

- Camp Lo dropped their Coolie High, Luchini and then released their first album, Uptown Saturday Night which put the fashioned-desi rappers on scene, incomparable to none.

- After releasing their fifth album, "The Love Movement," A Tribe Called Quest abruptly announce their breakup. Lead rapper Q-Tip immediately embarks on a solo career.

- Seeking a career rebirth, Snoop Dogg signs with Master P's No Limit label and rush-releases two lackluster albums.

- With a chain of restaurants, ("Justin's"), a clothing line, ("Sean John"), and a celebrity girlfriend, (Jennifer Lopez), Puff Daddy becomes the most recognized producer in hip-hop.

CHAPTER SEVEN
WHAT IS HIP HOP?
(REVISITED)

Hip-hop music is the vehicle of hip-hop culture and contains "rapping" (superimposed with vocals) by emcees. Inferable from this, hip-hop music is sometime alluded to as "rap music," However, the individuals who reject hip-hop as rap music don't fathom its rich history and the impact this classification of music has on youth.

Hip-hop music is a vehicle utilized by artists to address bigotry, mistreatment, and neediness issues. It describes stories of inward city African-Americans living the American dream from the base up, and harshly addresses racial segregation, broken homes, and conquering misfortune. Created by Jamaican vagrant DJ Kool Herc in the mid-70s in New York City, it has from that point forward spread its appendages over the world. Herc moved from reggae records to funk, shake and disco. Inferable from the short percussive breaks, he started broadening them utilizing a sound blender and two records.

As the remarkable style of music turned into a hit, performers (emcees) started superimposing the music with vocals; at first, they presented themselves as well as other people in the group of spectators. Afterward, the rapping turned out to be progressively differing, fusing brief rhymes, frequently with a sexual or brutal subject, trying to engage the group of spectators.

In the mid-1970s, hip-hop split into two gatherings. One concentrated on getting the group moving, another featured rapid-fire rhymes.

The 1980s saw a further enhancement in hip-hop; very figurative lyrics rapping over multi-layered beats supplanted basic vocals. During the 90s, gangsta rap (celebrated bandit way of life) moved toward becoming standard. Hip-hop was soon a necessary part of standard music, and about all the pop melodies highlighted a hidden component of hip-hop.

During the 90s and into the next decade, components of hip-hop were coordinated into differing classes of music: hip-hop soul joined hip-hop and soul music; in the Dominican Republic, an account by Santi Y Sus Duendes and Lisa M was begotten "Meren-rap," a combination of hip-hop and meringue. In Europe, Africa, and Asia, hip-hop has experienced progress from an underground event to the standard market.

Hip Hop gives point by point information on Hip Hop, Hip Hop And Rap, Hip Hop Music, R&B Hip Hop and these are just the beginning. Hip Hop affiliated with Karaoke Music Hip-hop is something other than music. The term incorporates an entire culture, and that clarifies how it has turned out to be a standout amongst the most compelling components molding global entertainment and youth self-expression. Everywhere throughout the world hip-hop is a device for clarifying the complexities of day by day life and speaking truth to control, whether through spoken lyrics, graffiti, art, dance or circle racer dominance. Not to be mistaken for business rap which frequently praises material overabundance, brutality, and misogyny—hip-hop was conceived in the South Bronx, New York, more than 40 years prior as an option in contrast to reckless pack culture. Hip-hop gave offended youth in devastated neighborhoods a chance to channel their dissatisfactions into art as opposed to brutality.

Hip hop music is part of hip hop culture predominately among African Americans and Latinos (the other two components are spray painting art and breakdancing). The explanations behind the ascent in hip hop music are found in the changing urban culture in the United States in the 1970s. Starting in the 1980s, hip hop culture started its spread over the world. By setting aside the effort to clarify a ripe culture articulation, understudies of hip hop music place available to us the absolute most interesting examinations of a ground-breaking art form. More than a musical style, hip-hop is a past filled with American culture and a declaration by its artists of their background. In 1985, when Run-DMC appointed themselves the "Lords of Rock," in the lyrics of their hit melody of a similar name, they likely never envisioned that one day they would be perceived all things considered. As the pioneers of hip-hop music, they persuaded the world to dance to verse with a beatbox. They welcomed any individual who might tune in to "Walk This Way" in "My Adidas," right to the highest priority on VH1's rundown of the 50 Greatest Hip-Hop Artists.

The lyrics found in hip hop music are articulations that are connected with social and societal sentiments of a person. Hip hop lyrics are known for their conversational quality. Hip hop lyrics are utilized to show expressive highlights, symbolism, sound similarity, similar sounding word usage, cadenced structure, and rhyme are educated while essential proficiency (vowels, consonants, mixes, syllables, and spelling) is implanted.

Hip hop lyrics ordinarily utilize internal city slang with lovely gadgets, for example, similar sounding word usage, sound similarity, and rhyme. The slang of hip hop lyrics may incorporate words like, yo, dis, stream, phat and homie. Hip hop lyrics have been compared to what shake music lyrics used to be, and sometimes have replaced shake and society melodies inside the culture. Hip hop lyrics contain numerous references that the audience members can identify with. Hip hop lyrics that recount overabundance riches and extravagance of artists may interface with a gathering of people with such dreams. As in the language, hip hop lyrics are verse, however, verse with something more added to it. Some hip hop lyrics are incredibly articulate in that they express a specific subject in an alternate form. Even though the facts confirm that numerous hip hop lyrics are slang it is likewise evident that quite a bit of our normal spoken language is slang and once in a while profane. Subsequently, enabling us to see that there is a contrast among distinct and prescriptive language. Adding to the hip hop music and tune lyrics, moving is another component of the hip hop culture otherwise called the hip hop dance style. Hip hop dance is a collective development that consistently develops and advances through individual spontaneous creation. Hip hop dance is an art form that has the country and world attempting to one-two stage or breakdance to krumping.

Hip hop music and moving, or breaking, ascended in the 1970s and 1980s, fixated on urban networks of youthful dancers and musicians and their pop culture. Hip hop moving keeps on developing into various forms today, intensely impacted by the advancement of music and its fame in the media. Hip-hop is a strenuous dance style that includes utilizing the whole body to make sharp, expressive developments. As in all dance forms, hip hop dance is a system with characterized steps and developments that must be learned and rehearsed.

Hip hop music is a famous style of music. It is wherever

from plugs to TV sitcoms. Hip hop culture and music go from those much the same as standard prevalent music to the blues form of the human condition. There is a major impact of R&B in the hip hop music industry that gives a thrilling knowledge to the audience. This urban culture is clearing the world in music, motion pictures, and clubs. It is an American minority creation which merits more acknowledge and acknowledgment as an art form as opposed to as a trend which should simply blur away with time.

CHAPTER EIGHT
HIP HOP AND THE YOUTH

Violence in rap isn't full of a feeling operator that takes steps to hurt America's youth; rather, it is the objection of an effectively existing issue from youth whose world views have been formed by encountering profound economic disparities separated to a great extent along racial lines. The agnostic way to deal with violence and crime for which rap is regularly censured is protected by certain craftsmen as the reasonable aftereffect of the variations that face African-American communities, from which rap began and remained established.

America's latest enumeration announced that African-American youth are the in all likelihood bunch in the country to live in poor family units and neighborhoods, to be jobless, to be the casualties of manslaughter or AIDS, or to invest energy in jail sooner or later in their lifetimes. For some poor, inward city youth, the weapon, which has had a focal job in the verses of numerous gangsta rappers, speaks to an approach to enable oneself and increase regard inside proceeding with cycles of racial and economic preference. Moreover, a few rappers protect the nearness of violence in their verses as the manifestation of American history and culture. By indicating rap as the reason for violence, government officials endeavor to eradicate from the cognizance of their constituents the historical backdrop of abuse that has brought forth hip-hop culture.

In request to really change the approaching nearness of violence in American society, as symptomized by violence in motion pictures, television, and music, the rest of the issues of destitution and bias in America's urban communities must be forcefully tended to. Amusingly, huge numbers of similar legislators and gatherings who shout out against violence in rap music are additionally driving the assault on Welfare, Affirmative Action, subsidizing for instruction, and recommendations for all-inclusive medicinal services. It is inconsistencies in financial and political power, not hip-hop music, that make violence in American society. Cutting programs that provide social administrations to help reduce the unequal opportunity to employment, assets, and social versatility will just serve to exasperate issues. Voters must not enable themselves to be tricked into accepting that censorship can safe-monitor kids from the repercussions of violence in American culture; they should not play into the issue by cutting programs that provide hope for departure from financial and political disparities that feed into the cycle of violence. Instead, the individuals who wish to put a conclusion to the issues communicated by certain rappers in their verses and ways of life must concentrate on giving administrations and openings that will battle the sentiment of agnosticism in a significant number of America's people group today. Social administrations must be upheld, extended, and redesigned to all the more successfully oversee programs for the individuals who have been financially and politically distraught. It is important to address the essential needs of the regular urban workers - moderate lodging, human services, and sustenance - before there can be any endeavors to take out violence in America's urban areas.

Furthermore, it is essential that regular workers grown-ups can gain a living compensation before they may start to be required to have hope for their future or the fate of their youngsters. The lowest pay permitted by law, as it exists today, isn't a sufficient family wage, and, subsequently, numerous guardians have been compelled to maintain a few sources of income, fending off them from home, to provide for their kids and relatives. At last, to forestall violence and wrongdoing before it starts, government, state, and nearby financing ought to be occupied from law authorization and jail frameworks into government funded training and youth programs. Youth can't have hope except if they approach a helpful, important instruction that can provide them with the opportunity to pick the way of their fates. I accept that couple of youth, given adequate assets, regard, and backing would pick violence. In any case, for some youth today, alternatives are constrained by a difference of access to the assets that provide that decision.

For some youth, the legends and success accounts of the inward city are rappers. The prevalence of rap and the turn off of hip-hop culture- - style lines like FUBU and Tommy Hilfiger, motion pictures, for example, Boyz N Da Hood and Friday, and television shows like The Fresh Prince of Bel-Air and In the House- - have majorly affected American promoting patterns.

The intrigue of hip-hop culture has pushed out of urban territories and into suburbia. Hip-hop has affected standard design, television, films, publicizing, and language Hoping to pursue the success of rappers like LL Cool J, Will Smith, Sean "Puffy" Combs, and Wyclef, numerous youth consider them to be industry as one of their solitary chances to accomplish the reputation and cash to get away from the hopelessness of the internal city. Nonetheless, the individuals who endeavor to prevail in hip-hop music face a troublesome test. In an industry constrained by for the most part by high society white men, youthful, urban minority musicians are frequently treated as products, not as specialists. They should adjust a requirement for aesthetic control and "keepin' it real" with the confinements and weights from record organizations keen on producing deals and huge intrigue. Regularly the message and imaginative respectability of rappers can be lost in the midst of national showcasing efforts and worry for endorsement by significant business partners, for example, Wal-Mart and MTV.

In the developing success of the hip-hop showcase, musicians have attempted to keep up rap's intensity as a form of opposition and strengthening. To safeguard rap's social capacity and, all the while, to advance masterful and business advance, the networks that have generally been the ones making the music ought to be the ones that control its generation and dispersion.

Hip-hop must be perceived as a musical form and not just a business pattern. Hip-hop, including its history, its forms, and its social significance, ought to be educated in school music education programs close by traditional music, people music, and jazz. The incorporation of rap in music instruction programs may likewise enable understudies and instructors to have open discussions on related issues, for example, the relationship among rap and posses, the nearness of violence, misogyny, and homophobia in some rap tunes, and the discussion over musical rating and warning frameworks.

Hip-hop ought to be grasped in state-funded school music programs as an American development and an approach to relate understudy interests with educational modules. Moreover, rap could be coordinated into English and language expressions educational modules as a form of both verse and show. Enabling understudies to compose and perform their own rap urges them to think basically, to work on writing in the account form, to build vocabulary, and to build up a comprehension of rhyme and musicality. Internal city youth associations, for example, the Boys and Girls Club or the YMCA, can execute programs that advance enthusiasm for hip-hop music. These associations give youth the order, self-assurance, leadership, and different instruments essential for success in the music industry. They might most likely work with nearby radio and television stations and record marks - particularly those began and claimed by African-Americans, for example, Def Jam and Bad Boy- - to provide open doors for internships, visits, and employment shadow days that give youth involvement in the music industry. They may enable youth to sort out, advance, and perform in hip-hop shows held routinely at the club. Including youth at all dimensions of arranging provides an important experience that engages them in the music industry and different aspects of the business.

Eventually, by enabling youth to see and experience how hip-hop is formed, contrarily and decidedly, by the matter of the music industry, they have the learning to settle on informed musical choices and, potentially, to make a change in the activities of the music industry.

CHAPTER NINE
CULTURE OF HIP HOP AND SOCIAL CONSCIOUSNESS

As of late, debate encompassing rap music has been in the cutting edge of the American media. From the promotion of the East Coast-West Coast contention that shadowed the killings of rappers Tupac Shakur and Notorious B.I.G. to the vilification of modem music in the wake of acts of mass violence in Littleton, Colorado, it appears that political and media gatherings have rushed to place fault on rap for an appearing pattern in youth brutality. In any case, however pundits rush to call attention to the rough verses of certain rappers; they are overlooking what's important of rap's message.

Rap, as different types of music, can't be comprehended except if it is contemplated without the edge of its recorded and social setting. The present rap music mirrors its starting point in the hip-hop culture of youthful, urban, average workers African-Americans, its foundations in the African oral custom, its capacity as the voice of a generally under-represented gathering, and, as its notoriety has developed, its commercialization and assignment by the music industry. Hip-hop music is commonly considered to have been spearheaded in New York's South Bronx in 1973 by Jamaican-conceived Kool DJ Herc. At a Halloween dance gathering tossed by his more youthful sister, Herc utilized an inventive turntable system to extend a song's drum break by playing the break segment of two indistinguishable records continuously. The fame of the all-encompassing break loaned its name to "breakdancing"- - a style explicit to hip-hop culture, which was encouraged by expanded drum breaks played by DJs at New York dance parties. By the mid-1970s, New York's hip-hop scene was ruled by original turntablists, DJ Grandmaster Flash, Afrika Bambaataa, and Herc. The rappers of Sugarhill Gang created hip-hop's first industrially effective hit, "Rapper's Delight," in 1979'.

Rap itself- - the rhymes expressed over hip-hop music- - started as an editorial on the capacity or abilities of a specific DJ while that DJ was playing records at a hip-hop occasion. MCs, the precursors of the present rap artists, presented DJs and their songs and frequently perceived the nearness of companions in the crowd at hip-hop exhibitions. Their job was cut out by well known African-American radio plate maneuvers in New York during the late 1960s, who presented songs and artists with unconstrained rhymes. The development of MCs grabbed the eye of hip-hop fans. Their rhymes lapped over from the change time frame between the finish of one song and the acquaintance of the following with the songs themselves. Their analyses moved exclusively from a DJ's abilities to their very own encounters and stories. The job of MCs in exhibitions climbed relentlessly, and they started to be perceived as artists in their very own right. The neighborhood prevalence of the cadenced music served by DJs at dance parties and clubs joined with an expansion in 'b-young men'- breakdancers and spray painting artists and the developing significance of MCs made a particular culture known as hip-hop.

Generally, hip-hop culture was characterized and grasped by youthful, urban, common laborers African-Americans. Hip-hop music started from a mix of generally African-American types of music- - including jazz, soul, gospel, and reggae. It was made by regular workers African-Americans, who, like Herc, exploited accessible apparatuses - vinyl records and turntables- - to develop another type of music that both communicated and molded the culture of dark New York City youth during the 1970s.

While rap's history seems brief its connection to the African oral tradition, which furnishes rap with quite a bit of its present social importance, likewise roots rap in a long-standing history of oral students of history, melodious fetishism, and political promotion. At the core of the African oral tradition is the West African3 thought of nommo. In Malian Dogon cosmology, Nommo is the main human, a making of the incomparable divinity, Amma, whose imaginative power lies in the generative property of the spoken word4. As a philosophical idea, nommo is the animative capacity of words and the conveyance of words to follow up on items, giving life. The centrality of nommo in the African oral tradition has offered the capacity to rappers and rap music inside numerous African-American communities.

Rap's normal assignment as "CNN for dark individuals" may result from the descendence of rappers from griots, regarded African oral history specialists and acclaim vocalists. Griots were the guardians and purveyors of information, including innate history, family heredity, and updates on births, passings, and wars. Voyaging griots spread learning in an available form- - the verbally expressed word- - to individuals from ancestral towns. So also, in the United States, numerous rappers make songs that, through performances and records, spread updates on their day by day lives, dreams, and discontents outside of their prompt neighborhoods.

Rappers are seen as the voice of poor, urban African-American youth, whose lives are commonly rejected or distorted by the predominant press. They are the attendants of contemporary African-American average workers history and concerns. Furthermore, rap's potential for political support comes from the capacity of its antecedents, African-American rhyming diversions, as forms of protection from frameworks of enslavement and servitude. Rhyming games encoded race relations between African-American slaves and their white experts in a manner that enabled them to pass the investigation of suspicious managers. Furthermore, rhyming diversions enabled captives to utilize their inventive mind to give motivation and stimulation. For instance, by describing the slave as a bunny and the ace as a fox, "Brer Rabbit stories" camouflaged accounts of slaves outmaneuvering their lords and getting away ranches behind the veneer of a funny experience.

Hip-hop writer, Davey D associates the African oral tradition to present day rap: "You see, the slaves were brilliant and they talked in similitudes. They would be executed if the slave bosses heard them talking in new tongues. So they did what advanced rappers do- - they flexed their melodious skillz."

Rap has created as a form of protection from the oppression of common laborers African-Americans in urban focuses. Despite the fact that it might be seen essentially as a form of amusement, rap has the ground-breaking potential to address social, economic, and political issues and go about as a bringing together voice for its group of spectators. Rap imparts its underlying foundations to different forms of traditionally African-American music, for example, jazz, blues, and soul. Rap may likewise be firmly connected to reggae music, a sort that additionally created from the blend of traditional African drumming and the music of the European decision class by the youth of constrained economic methods inside an arrangement of African economic oppression. In an amusing circle of impact, Jamaican reggae was played on African-American radio stations in New York during the 1960s. DJs utilized rhymes to present reggae songs. These stations could be gotten in Jamaica, where audience members grabbed on the DJs' rhyming styles, extending them over reggae songs to make "name"- - another precursor of rap.

Kool DJ Herc, before presenting his creative turntable style, brought his name style to New York, yet it neglected to pick up notoriety. He focused on building up his DJing abilities, which later took into consideration the acknowledgment of MCing and, in the long run, rap.

The advancement of rap and reggae has been an interlaced way of two distinct styles, which have developed from and have flourished, in comparative conditions. At long last, similarly, as reggae has been enduring an onslaught for certain craftsmen's appearing promotion of violence to unravel social, political, and economic issues, rap has turned into the substitute of the American musical texture, as it, as well, has confronted mass prevalence and commercialization. Similarly, as reggae is currently under danger of losing its capacity as a work of art and a social voice" in the wake of being appropriated by those outside of the Rastafarian culture, rap battles to endure reception and commodification by that outside of the universe of hip-hop.

In recent decades, hip-hop music has pursued the way of commercialization that wrecked African-American radio stations in the 1970s. Though preceding commercialization, African-American proprietors, software engineers, and DJs had the opportunity to utilize their stations to serve the particular needs of their audience members - New York's average worker's African-American community. They had the option to advance nearby craftsmen and occasions and to address news occasions and social worries as individuals from a similar community from which they drew their group of spectators. Nonetheless, as enterprises claimed by businessmen outside of the community united power by buying nearby stations, African-American AM stations were constrained out of the market by more economically-ground-breaking stations possessed and controlled principally by individuals from the white high society. African - American DJs lost their influence as the cutting edge griots of their communities and as the moderators of hip-hop music and culture. Similarly, with the revelation of hip-hop craftsmen by corporate record names, rap music was stolen from its community, repackaged by cash disapproved of businessmen hoping to make a more extensive intrigue by eradicating hip-hop's memorable capacity, and sold back to the avenues through showcasing ploys, for example, music recordings and Top-40 outlines.

By the 1980s, hip-hop had turned into a business and rap music was an important product and rap's commodification has likewise disappointed it as a form of obstruction. Corporate America's fixation on rap has expanded as the class' political substance has wilted. Ice Cube's initial songs assaulted white bigotry; Ice-T sang a song about a cop executioner; Public Enemy moved audience members to "fight the power." In any case, numerous more up to date acts are centered on the whole around pathologies inside the black community. They now rap about shooting different blacks, yet never about testing legislative expert or empowering social activism. In spite of the fact that not new topics, huge numbers of the parts of rap that have been brought up by government officials as "frightful"- - violence, misogyny, and homophobia in the verses and ways of life of certain rappers- - might be viewed as a component of rap's commodification. While rappers battle to "keep it real"- - a term which reminds those inside hip-hop to be consistent with their underlying foundations - some concede that numerous rappers do as their record marks wish- - just, they compose verses that are permitted. In a group of people which has moved toward becoming progressively ethnically and economically different, business-disapproved of rappers have been compelled to take on the restricted jobs that have demonstrated beneficial for youthful; African-American male specialists - that of the "pimp," the "gangsta", and the "playa." The commodification of rap has permitted huge checks and platinum records to eradicate the verifiable, social, and economic settings, out of which rap has developed, from open cognizance. As indicated by Davey D, "The matter of music has degraded rap." from its foundations as opposition against servitude to its association with the reggae development in Jamaica to the presence of rappers as cutting edge griots, rap has traditionally been the music of the enslaved African-American common laborers.

While it is critical to commend hip-hop culture today as comprehensive of incomprehensibly different ethnic and economic gatherings, it is similarly imperative to perceive and protect the capacity that rap has served for its unique community. So as to comprehend the subjects and forms of rap music, it is essential to pursue the history of African-Americans from their beginnings in West Africa, to their subjugation all through the early history of the United States, to their battles against racial preference and isolation after Emancipation, to the proceeding with fights against true economic isolation and recovery of social personality of numerous African-Americans today. In the event that rap music gives off an impression of being too much rough when contrasted with nation western or mainstream shake, it is on the grounds that rap comes from a culture that has been leaked in the battle against political, social, and economic persecution. Notwithstanding the showy behavior now and then put on for real mark collections or MTV videos, for some, specialists, rapping about guns and drug life is an impression of day by day life in racially-and economically-stratified internal city ghettos and lodging ventures.

CHAPTER TEN
HIP HOP IMPACTING ALL

UNIFICATION AND EDUCATION

One of these positive impacts is that it has been used as an incredible unifier of various populaces around the globe. It began as a subculture among African American communities in America yet it is presently a wonder of worldwide culture. In actuality, it isn't just confined to African American communities, as communities of color contain seventy-five percent of the worldwide hip hop group of spectators. The way that hip hop has crossed the social separation exhibits its capacity to bring together a large number of youth around the world. This is reminiscent of when shake music was on everybody's lips universally. The development of hip hop culture is conspicuous in the urban road style of dressing duplicated from hip hop artists. The trademark highlights of this style are loose jeans, tops worn in reverse just as costly tennis shoes, which gives young people a feeling of character. Hip hop has been crucial in advancing social and political mindfulness among the youth of today. Hip hop music teaches individuals from a few alternate points of view and raises numerous social issues. Hip hop is a channel for individuals to talk unreservedly about their view on political or social issues and like this, it draws in youngsters to wind up concerned and mindful of these issues. This is significant in making the youth mindful of their general surroundings and the conditions they face in the public eye, empowering people to talk about manners by which they can roll out a positive improvement inside society. A couple of the issues that hip hop has made mindfulness in racial separation, distinction and the significance of training and putting stock in your fantasies. Hip hop additionally is an impression of the spirit and mind and is a comfort for both the artists and audience members who might battle with similar issues. Music, as a rule, unites individuals, however, the youth of today can identify with the battle and challenges that most rappers talk about. Since the arrival of Grandmaster Flash's "The Message" in 1982, hip hop music has received an increasingly political tone. Hip hop music, more than some other classification, has cautioned both private and open residents of the predicament of the lower classes in urban zones among different issues. Some hip-hoppers are known for their dubious verses can frequently point out more noteworthy issues.

HOPE

Many rappers rap about destitution and their battles in inward city America while growing up. When they make progress, they talk about conquering hindrances and ascending to the top. This message can give hope to numerous youths crosswise over America who live in comparable conditions. For instance, when a rapper raps about his tested youth or about prevailing regardless of living with a medication dependent parent, an adolescent in a comparable circumstance may accept that he, as well, can get past his battles.

SOCIAL AWARENESS

Through training and understanding, hip hop music has impelled social mindfulness in communities around the nation. Hip hop music has filled in as an apparatus to stand in opposition to negative parts of life, for example, brutality and firearms. Numerous artists use their musical abilities to advance harmony and hostile to rough acts. By imparting messages about brutality and separation, and identifying with youth individuals, it gives a chance to them to roll out positive improvements in their own life. Rappers, for example, the late Tupac Shakur were frequently reprimanded for their verses, which illustrated urban America. While such verses were maybe somewhat expected to stun buyers, they additionally carried attention to the nation's social problems, especially those in the inward city. Issues, for example, viciousness, illicit drug use, and destitution are on the whole normal topics in hip hop music. When somebody tunes in to the class, he might do as such for stimulation, however, he won't most likely abstain from finding out about these issues and offering thought to them. There is some hip hop music that is made with the expectation of sending a positive message to its group of spectators. There are melodies that reprove viciousness and call for more harmony and fellowship in the inward city trying to improve personal satisfaction. One incredible case of a rap melody that sends this message is entitled "Implosion" and performed by the East Coast All Stars. Presently for you Hip-Hop students of history, I realize this returns a long while, however it is a standout amongst the best instances of the positive impact of hip hop music. A gathering of free rap artists got together to make this tune because they knew about the extraordinary power and impact that they have with their music and were endeavoring to use that impact to roll out a positive improvement. This venture filled two significant needs because it didn't just make consciousness of the internal city's problems with viciousness, however, it additionally demonstrated that rappers could be socially cognizant and make music that was positive.

OFFERING HELP

When managing social problems, a standout amongst the most significant methods for finding an answer for the issue is to make others inside our general public mindful of it. Hip hop music is an incredible instrument for encouraging that procedure because of its fame; it can carry a message to the majority. By far, most of the rap artists are from inner cities where below average social conditions and imbalance can be seen the most. Ordinarily, when a rapper composes a melody that discusses savagery, sedate use or other criminal activity, it is because it is something that they have found in their living condition and this manner are in a decent position to give a point by point record of how life is there. A few rappers may confess to taking an interest in a portion of the previously mentioned activity however once more, isn't constantly imply that they are commending it. A specific story might be advised to give hope and let an audience realize that because they have committed errors previously, it doesn't imply that they can't change their life and be engaged with something positive. The rappers use their music to bring issues to light of these issues with the goal that some center can be put into improving them.

ENTERTAINMENT

Hip hop music's universally useful is to engage its crowd. Because a rapper paints themselves in an image of being related in criminal activity, burning through a large number of dollars on apparently pointless things or having intercourse with different ladies doesn't imply that they really do. On numerous events, the rap craftsman is making a fictionalized record of specific occasions for the reason for charming and engaging individuals and now and again uses characters to encourage those records. A portion of the more capable rappers can use their words to make these characters alongside striking storylines that frequently are identified with an urban topic. This is the same as different types of stimulation, specifically, the film business. When we watch our preferred on-screen character conveying and utilizing their firearms to slaughter individuals, devouring medications, or being depicted exceedingly explicitly in a film, it isn't viewed as a ruffian. A portion of the characters being made in these motion pictures is the same than a portion of the characters that are made in hip hop music. Because a rapper says that they do certain things in their music, it doesn't imply that they generally do. While the pictures that are displayed in some rap music can surely be viewed as an awful impact, it doesn't imply that all hip hop music is degenerate. Is it degenerate when holy places use Christian rap in their administration to communicate something specific? Is it degenerate when cops, firemen, and instructors use it to spread their message and endeavor to make an association with the youth?

PROGRAMS

Rap music is an extraordinary and incredible asset that can be used for good purposes. When evaluating rap music, one needs to go past the outside of what they are hearing and endeavor to learn the message that the music is endeavoring to send. Projects Rap and hip hop are being used inside the social work field as a type of therapy. Hip-Hop Therapy uses hip hop culture and music to draw in youth and address their issues in therapy. The objective is to get youth patients to think about their past encounters by interfacing with hip hop lyrics. Recently grassroots associations have jumped up in the United States that plan to use hip hop and rap to diminish youth savagery. In Tucson, Arizona, Usiel Barrios has made basic Hip Hop Skool, which plans to use hip hop to get youngsters engaged with network building. This program intends to engage youngsters with leadership abilities, support positive self-articulation, and advance network contribution – through hip hop. Another grassroots association that has been made as of late is, Project Spitfire. This association was established by Henry Mann and means to combine youthful musicians with expert makers who help them record melodies and recordings. Firecracker additionally gives artists a $100 marking reward, photography shoots, and exposure. Firecracker expects to sign youthful artists who talk about change and options. They will likely sign artists who can show the youth that there are options in contrast to packs and savagery. Mann needs to give youthful rappers a road to recount to their accounts and past lived encounters in the hope that it will impact change in the youth culture.

AFTERWORD

Hip Hop has moved past it humble beginnings in the South Bronx and all through street corners and arranged spaces in American culture and culture. It has moved from negligible verses and basement parties to issues in presidential discussions and sentiments, just as, in each dimension of the legal executive. It is the subject matter of children's' storybooks to all things considered for doctorates. Hip Hop holdings and accumulations are in exhibition halls at Harvard University to pretty much every community library in the country.

The culture of Hip Hop is as yet alive on the streets and in tha' 'hood as much for what it's worth in the institute. From its refusal to being on MTV to getting to be one of the biggest broad communications and promoting 'item,' hip hop is solid and frail in various ways. It is implanted in American culture on all coasts and from mean-street to

AFTERWORD

fundamental street. As much as it is grounded, it is extraterrestrial - compliments of NASA.

Hip Hop as a worldwide wonder is verifiable, and as a social and corporate power, it is a seething bull. It is one of the major sociological occasions and subjects of this modern era and it merits expanding consideration in the speculations and investigations of the sociologies and humanities. Its traces have expanded as the writings have created.

Hip Hop is absolutely not traditional but rather a missional emanation of having a contract for the cultures of the seized. It's a human science as much as a sociological viewpoint on urban culture.

www.ingramcontent.com/pod-product-compliance
Lightning Source LLC
Chambersburg PA
CBHW021051080526
44587CB00010B/210